manifesto

I0022963

Marx's *Das Kapital* and capitalism today
Robert Griffiths

This second edition updates the complete work first published in 2018
by Manifesto Press and revised from a version previously serialised in 2017
in *Communist Review*
© Robert Griffiths

All rights reserved. Apart from fair dealing, e.g. for the purpose of private study
or research, no part of this publication may be reproduced or transmitted,
in any form or by any means, electronic, photocopying, recording or otherwise,
without the prior permission of the copyright owner.
All rights reserved

ISBN 978-1-907464-36-2
Typset in Bodoni and Gill
Images Wikimedia Commons

Contents

ii   **Glossary**
iii   **Foreword**

1   **1 The capitalist mode of production**

The first draft of *Capital*
- Commodities, value and exploitation
- Working class women
- 'Estrangement' (or alienation)
- Cyclical crises
- Capital accumulation and the 'reserve army'
- 'Primitive accumulation'
- Concentration, centralisation, globalisation
- 'Pauperisation' — absolute and relative
- Political Economy in the battle of ideas
- 'Productive' and 'unproductive' labour
- Crises of disproportion
- The 'price of production'
- The tendency of the rate of profit to fall
- Piketty versus *Capital*
- Theoretical controversies
- 'Under-consumption' and Keynesianism
- Monetarism and neo-liberalism
- 'Fictitious' capital, financialisation and the 'Great Crash'
- A 'green' Marx?

58   **2 The commmunist mode of production**

Marx and the future society
- The Soviet Union and the Law of Value
- Socialism or 'state capitalism'?
- 'Socialism with Chinese characteristics'
- Cooperation and cooperatives
- Lessons for the future

82   **Notes**
90   **Index**

Glossary

ACCPE	*A Contribution to the Critique of Political Economy*
COMECON	Council for Mutual Economic Assistance
CPC	Communist Party of China
CPSU	Communist Party of the Soviet Union
EU	European Union
GDP	gross domestic product
GDR	German Democratic Republic
GNP	gross national product
HMRC	Her Majesty's Revenue and Customs
ILO	International Labour Organisation
IMF	International Monetary Fund
IWMA	International Working Men's Association
M&As	mergers and acquisitions
MCC	Mondragon Cooperative Corporation
OCC	organic composition of capital
OECD	Organisation for Economic Co-operation and Development
ONS	Office for National Statistics
TNC	transnational corporation
TRPF	tendency for the rate of profit to fall
TSSI	Temporal Single-System Interpretation
TUC	Trades Union Congress
UN	United Nations

Robert Griffiths is general secretary of the Communist Party of Britain and formerly a TUC tutor and senior lecturer in Labour History and Political Economy at University of Wales College, Newport. He gained a BSc (hons) in Economics & Administration at the University of Bath. His previous books include *SO Davies — A Socialist Faith* (1983), *Streic! Streic! Streic! (1986)*, *Driven by ideals — a history of ASLEF* (2005), *Killing no murder: South Wales and the Great Railway Strike of 1911* (2009) *and Granite and honey: the story of Phil Piratin, Communist MP* (2012) with Kevin Marsh.

Foreword

This is a revised, updated and extended edition of a book first produced in April 2018. The original was based on a series of three articles published in the Communist Party's theoretical and discussion journal *Communist Review* in 2017-18.

As for the first edition, my thanks are due to *Communist Review* editor Martin Levy and Manifesto Press editor Nick Wright for their assistance and advice, and to Michael Roberts for permission to reproduce material from his highly informative blog site. This second edition also includes some new or expanded points in response to helpful comments received from Jonathan White, Martin Levy and Steve Bell.

Nonetheless, responsibility for the contents of this book is solely mine.

Robert Griffiths
Cardiff
October 2018

Das Kapital.

Kritik der politischen Oekonomie.

von

Karl Marx.

Erster Band.

Buch I: Der Produktionsprocess des Kapitals.

Das Recht der Uebersetzung wird vorbehalten.

Hamburg

Verlag von Otto Meissner.

1867.

New-York: L. W. Schmidt. 24 Barclay-Street.

∎ The capitalist mode of production

THE FIRST volume of *Capital* by Karl Marx was published in 1867, in German as *Das Kapital*. It bore the fruit of ten years of study, analysis and composition in the wake of the first real international crisis of capitalism.

his work began in earnest with his *Economic Manuscripts of 1857-58*.[1] In essence, these represent the first draft of Volume I of *Capital*.

Portions of the *Economic Manuscripts* on the dual character and values of commodities, labour and money were then restructured and published in 1859 as 'part one' of *A Contribution to the Critique of Political Economy* (ACCPE).[2] The title was to become the sub-title of *Capital* proper. In a famous preface to the 1859 text, Marx summarised his theory of historical materialism, with its revolutionary conclusion that within each mode of production (whether slavery, feudalism or capitalism), society's productive forces develop to the point where the existing relations between the exploiting and exploited classes act as an absolute barrier to their further development and so have to be ruptured: 'Then begins an era of social revolution'.[3]

Although ACCPE launched a fierce assault on classical bourgeois political economy's understanding of value, labour and money, it met initially with silence in Germany. But German-speaking workers there and in émigré communities in France, England and the USA awoke to the significance of its contents, not least its exposition of the Theory of Labour Exploitation.

Family illness and an upsurge in working class and national-democratic movements in Germany, Italy and Poland and the American Civil War interrupted Marx's efforts to complete the second part of ACCPE. What he produced in the end was the *Economic Manuscript of 1861-63*, in effect the second draft of Volume I of *Capital*.[4] Additional notebooks and the *Economic Manuscript of 1863-65* followed, on which Marx worked intermittently until his death in 1883. Other commitments — not least his leading role in the International Working Men's Association (the IWMA or 'First International') from 1864 until 1873 — meant that it was only in 1885 and 1894 that much of this material was published, as Volumes II and III respectively of *Capital*, prepared and edited by Frederick Engels. A hitherto unpublished section of the *1861-63 Manuscript*, 'Theories of Surplus Value', was later produced by Karl Kautsky, although a complete and accurate translation did not follow until 1963-71.

The first draft of *Capital*

In August 1857, US investors had begun to lose confidence in insurance companies, banks and railroad stocks after an economic boom based on the expansion of international trade, gold discoveries and credit-fuelled investment and speculation. The panic provoked a financial crash with banking and insurance failures and cutbacks in production. Extensive US commercial and financial links spread the impact to parts of Western Europe, the Far East, Australia and Latin America. In

Britain, financial institutions involved in the extensive trade with the US collapsed, contributing to an economic stagnation that lasted until late in 1858.[5]

While politicians, economists and commentators in Britain pinned the blame for this first major international crisis on over-speculation, unsound credit, inadequate gold supply, the Crimean War or on some permutation of them, Marx located the root of the crisis in capitalism's cyclical character. In a series of articles for the *New York Daily Tribune*, he argued that as the economy grows and accelerates, investment and production increase along with profit, credit and speculation.[6] Inevitably, a point is reached where there is an 'over-production' of commodities, not all of which can then be sold at a profit. It is in these conditions that investors, speculators and stock markets become nervous, more sensitive to signs of slowdown and failure. Production declines, investment is cut back, workers are laid off, prices and profits fall, stocks and shares go down, companies fail and the economy as a whole sinks into recession. Recovery will then occur as it becomes profitable once more to produce commodities with lower-cost premises, plant, machinery, supplies, labour and credit. The pace quickens, breaks into a boom and so the cycle proceeds.

While other factors — economic, political, legal — can hasten, postpone, aggravate or prolong capitalism's periodic crises, Marx suggested that their underlying and primary cause is to be found in the sphere of production. This remained the case, he argued, even though dramatic commercial and financial events had occupied the newspaper headlines, parliamentary speeches and the official reports in 1857-58.[7] Varying the amount of money in circulation beforehand, or curbing speculation on the stock exchange, might have affected the contours of the crisis in some way, but they would not have prevented it from breaking out sooner or later.

Marx's intention with his *Economic Manuscripts of 1857-58* was to help workers understand the laws and tendencies of the economic and political system in which they worked and lived, so that they would see why capitalism must be overthrown and replaced by communism. Six of the seven notebooks comprise a chapter on 'Capital', where he traced the development of trade, money and commodities. Capitalism is defined as a mode of production in which, firstly, most goods and services are produced for sale in a market, ie., as commodities. Indeed, as he was to put it later in Volume I proper of *Capital*, in terms of its material wealth capitalist society presents itself as 'an immense accumulation of commodities'.[8]

Secondly, the means of production (land, premises, plant and machinery, raw materials and other inputs, etc.) are largely in private ownership. Thirdly, labour power — the worker's capacity to work — has also become a universal commodity. In fact, without the purchase and application of labour power, the means of production could not be set in motion.

Commodities, value and exploitation

In the *1857-58 Manuscripts*, Marx transformed the Labour Theory of Value advanced by Adam Smith and David Ricardo — with all their confusions around wealth and value — into his own Theory of Labour Exploitation (or Theory of Surplus Value). In particular, he explained how workers are robbed of much of the value they produce. His main propositions had been amended and refined in a series of newspaper articles and then published together in 1849 under the title *Wage Labour and Capital*.

Every commodity must have 'use-value', so that a consumer wishes to buy it. But that cannot determine its price, nor does it explain why very different types of commodity in terms of their size, weight, composition, etc., can actually be measured against one another through their price (or 'exchange-value') on the market. The one characteristic all commodities have in common, to which they can all be reduced and by which their value can therefore be measured, is the labour time that goes into every aspect of their production. The past labour time embodied in the means of production used up in producing the commodity, together with the present or living labour time turning those means into the finished product, is the starting point for determining a commodity's exchange-value. It is why there is almost always a proportionality within limits between the prices of vastly different commodities. Obviously, market prices can be driven above or below a commodity's exchange-value due to factors of supply and demand, monopoly power, state regulation, etc., but these are fluctuations around that value and are rarely completely divorced from it.

When the average worker sells her or his labour time to the capitalist employer, what is its exchange-value? Like any other commodity, it is the average amount of society's labour time necessary to produce that commodity, to produce the means of consumption (accommodation, food, clothing, leisure etc.) that enable the worker and any dependants to live, work and rear the next generation of workers. Therefore, the worker's wage broadly reflects the value of her or his labour power.

But labour power has the capacity to produce more value in a day or a week than it needs to consume. As well as producing value equivalent to the value of the wage used to buy one day's worth of means of consumption, which might take five hours of labour time, the worker then goes on working for another, say, three, hours. This produces three hours of 'surplus value' in labour time for the capitalist employer, for which the worker is unpaid. But like the value of the five hours paid labour time and of the past labour time embodied in the means of production used up in producing the commodity, the value of this surplus labour time will be transferred into the total value of the end commodity and reflected in its selling price. The employer has not paid the worker in full for his or her eight hours of labour, with a wage worth eight hours of means of consumption. Instead, the employer has paid the worker in full for her or his capacity to work, ie., her or his labour power, which can be set to work on the means of production for eight hours a day. Of course, the wage is presented as full payment for the hours worked (or for the commodities produced in the case of piece-work), thereby concealing the unpaid surplus labour performed and the surplus value it has created.

Here is the great secret discovered by Marx and which had escaped earlier political economists. While the likes of Smith and Ricardo had acknowledged that, indeed, labour power is the one indispensable factor in the production of society's material wealth, their labour theories of value not only held that workers were fairly rewarded for their contribution. They also maintained that the normal sale price of a commodity also contained fair and proper returns to the owners of the other 'factors of production' besides labour: thus the owners of plant and machinery received profit on their capital employed, landowners received rent and financiers received interest.

Marx analysed the circuit of capital and the creation and distribution of value very differently.

The capitalist does not derive profit from the means of production that they own and which are used up in whole or part in creating the new commodity. When that commodity is sold at a price around its exchange-value, the capitalist gets back the money laid out on all the inputs (materials, power, etc.), including compensation for the depreciation of machinery, buildings, etc. Marx refers to that money as constant capital (c) because the value it represents remains constant. The value of the used-up means of production is merely transferred, unchanged, into the new commodity. It is cashed at the point of sale and reimburses the capitalist for the cost of those means of production.

Marx called the money laid out on living labour power — in the form of wages — variable capital (v), because it represents a value which varies, ie., increases, in the course of the production process. The labour power purchased at a price equivalent to five hours labour time creates eight hours of value, including three hours of surplus value (s). The total value of the final commodity is equivalent to $c + v + s$. The consumer pays the equivalent price, not only reimbursing the capitalist for the cost of means of production and labour power (c + v), but also providing the capitalist with a gross operating profit (s). Out of this last sum, the capitalist pays rent and interest, draws an income and can fund expansion over and above the replenishment of current levels of means of production and labour power through c + v.

Here is the 'use-value' of labour power as far as the capitalist is concerned: it produces surplus value, which from the standpoint of the capitalist is the only reason for producing anything. Under capitalism, commodities are not produced in order to make people happy, or to meet some pressing social need. As Marx put it in his *Economic Manuscript of 1861-63*: 'The direct purpose of capitalist production is not the production of commodities, but of surplus value or profit'.[9] Left to its own devices, capitalism would not produce anything that does not do so.

Recent calculations indicate that the rate of exploitation or surplus value (the proportion s/v) in Britain has ranged from 42% to 63% between 1986 and 2009.[10] In other words, the average production worker performs somewhere between 31/2 and 5 hours unpaid labour in an 8-hour day, not counting breaks. Michael Roberts estimates that exploitation rates varied from 42% to 68% in the US economy between 1945 and 2014.[11]

Because a commodity's surplus value does not manifest itself as extra money until the point of sale, the illusion is created that profit originates in the sphere of circulation — and then only in its final stage — rather than production.

As already noted, out of the surplus value other sections of the capitalist class may draw rent for land and interest on loan capital from the commodity producing capitalist. Rent and interest are also collected directly from workers by other capitalists, of course, and after the deduction of costs this is also classed as 'profit' in the everyday use of the term. Nonetheless, Marx made the important point that, however defined, the source of capitalist profit in general is not to be found in the spheres of circulation and finance as such, but in the sphere of the commodity production by living labour power.

Furthermore, while constant capital (c) replenishes the means of production at their previous level, a portion of the surplus value (s) is used to expand investment, production and therefore profit in a process of expanded reproduction. In this way, capital accumulates to exercise what Marx called its 'great civilising influence' by developing society's productive forces on a colossal scale.[12]

In presenting this Theory of Labour Exploitation, Marx also laid bare the motive for employers to maintain or even extend the working day or week. It would enable them to increase the absolute amount of unpaid labour time (ie., surplus value) extracted from the workers' labour power. Hence the capitalist resistance to trade union demands for the 8-hour day, the 5-day week and more holidays.

Guided and enthused by Marx, the IWMA in 1866 took up the demand for the 8-hour day; in 1889, the Second (Socialist) International made it the theme of the first-ever International Workers' Day demonstrations on May 1. Enacted first in Soviet Russia four days after the Great October Socialist Revolution in 1917, the 8-hour day was soon won by workers in France and Portugal and by railway workers in Britain after a nine-day strike in 1919.

Nevertheless, the struggle over the duration of working time has continued ever since. In 1989-90, the Confederation of Shipbuilding and Engineering Unions in Britain launched a rolling programme of subsidised, selective strikes to compel employers to reduce the standard working week from 39 hours to 35; numerous companies affiliated to the Engineering Employers Federation broke ranks to settle at 36-38 hours. In France, the Socialist-Communist coalition government legislated in 2000 for a universal 35-hour week. Today, most countries have national laws limiting the obligatory working week to 40-48 hours, but some have higher limits (Kenya) or none at all (Nigeria, India, Pakistan, Jamaica, Grenada), although in some of the latter there are limits agreed through collective bargaining with trade unions (Germany, Australia, Denmark) or within an international legislative framework such as the European Union's Working Time Directive. But weak enforcement, exempted occupations and 'voluntary' overtime mean that the struggle proposed by Marx and the IWMA continues and, as in France currently, employers and their hired politicians still strive to change the law to allow longer working time.

There are other ways in which employers seek to maximise surplus value. For example, working class consumption can be cut in real terms, hence in part the struggle over wages and payment systems. But this can be only be taken so far before it adversely affects the worker's capacity to work, produce value and to rear the next generation of labour power.

Surplus value can also be increased relatively, by reducing the value of labour power (v), so that less of the worker's labour time is required to earn the wage needed to purchase life's necessities. This is made possible by increasing productivity, especially in those branches producing consumer goods most required by the working class. Hence the struggle over the intensity of work and control of the work process. But higher productivity will only lower the average labour time necessary to produce the essentials of life for the average worker if it can be achieved in all the relevant branches of production.

Another possibility is to import cheaper consumer goods or their raw materials from outside. This option is, of course, limited by problems of availability and the willingness of importers to sell their commodities at significantly below the prevailing market price.

More recently, we have seen the spread of various forms of contracted labour in the guise of 'self-employment' in some of the developed capitalist economies, not least in Britain. The genuinely self-employed worker sells his or her commodity to the customer at more or less its value, in other words at a price that very roughly reflects the past and living labour time that has gone into its production (although the means of production have usually been secured at 'trade' discount below their value). There is no unpaid surplus labour time as such, because the self-employed worker is being paid for every hour worked. But the contractor of so-called 'self-employed' labour pays only for the hire of the labour power, often maximising the surplus value from it by not paying for holiday time, sickness, maternity or paternity leave, etc.

Such social and welfare benefits are part of what today — together with public services such as health, education, etc. — is regarded as the 'social wage'. Workers and capitalists fund it through taxation and state insurance rather than by payment at the point of delivery. It is in the interests of the working class to maximise the funding contribution from the capitalist class and enhance the 'social wage' in both quality and quantity, the capitalists seek to minimise their financial contribution while ensuring that those services essential to the functioning of capitalism and its workforce are maintained, preferably on a basis that also allows profits to be made. This struggle over the formation and composition of the social wage is today a prominent feature of the economic and political class struggle in capitalist society.

Working class women

For Marx, capitalism's tendency to break down handicraft manufacturing into separate tasks had lowered the value of the worker, who no longer had to develop and exercise a range of skills. The same process of deskilling had opened the workshop door to women and children. Yet, he noted with a hint of admiration, the skilled male operatives had stubbornly resisted this tendency with some success, for example through retention of the apprenticeship system.

However, a whole sub-section of Volume I of *Capital* explained how the subsequent replacement of heavy labour by machinery then enabled employers to take on large numbers of workers of less muscular strength but of greater suppleness. As Marx put it: 'By the excessive addition of women and children to the ranks of the workers, machinery at last breaks down the resistance which the male operatives in the manufacturing period continued to oppose to the despotism of capital'.[13] Thus, too, machinery swiftly became the means for 'enrolling, under the direct sway of capital, every member of the workman's family, without distinction of age or sex'. The division of labour becomes 'based, wherever possible, on the employment of women, of children of all ages, and of unskilled labourers, in one word, on cheap labour, as it is characteristically called in England'.[14] By the time of the 1861 census in England and Wales, women and girls constituted 38% of the industrial workforce in the factories, mills and foundries.[15] There were 202,000 children below the age of 15 working in the textile industries, just over half of them girls, and 19,000 less than 10 years old. Around 40,000 boys toiled in the coal mines and 19,500 in the iron and steel industry.[16]

As a consequence, Marx noted, 'Compulsory work for the capitalists usurped the place, not only of the children's play, but also of free labour at home within moderate limits for the support of the family'. Mirroring the position of skilled workers and their trades unions, he clearly approved of the contributions that women and daughters could make to home-life, sustaining and replenishing male labour power. Indeed, he noted some advantages of the idleness imposed on the Lancashire and Cheshire cotton workers by the American Civil War, in addition to fresh air away from the mills: mothers now had time to breastfeed their babies 'instead of poisoning them with Godfrey's "cordial"'; women were learning to cook — even though they had nothing to cook — and daughters were taught useful skills at sewing schools.[17] The widespread recruitment of women and girls into industry would permanently withdraw the time available for such domestic pursuits. Instead of doing their own sewing and mending, households would have to buy in ready-made articles, absorbing any extra income from outside employment. This growing dependency on their wages, together with the relative lightness of their machine work, contributed to what Marx called the 'more pliant and docile character' of women and child workers.[18]

Furthermore, Marx explained how large-scale expansion of the industrial workforce cheapened the value of labour power: where once a single day's wage would maintain a family of four in return for one day's labour power, henceforth, for little more than the equivalent of one day's wage, four days' labour power could be purchased and with it four portions of surplus labour. Thus was raised the general rate of exploitation. The capitalist buys underage youngsters and, where previously the workman sold his own labour power, 'now he sells his wife and child, He has become a slave-dealer'. Although he recognised that male operatives had campaigned for shorter hours for women and child workers, wanting them back in the home, Marx was scathing about the 'revolting' conduct of some parents in the 'traffic in children'. Then there was the 'Pharisee of a capitalist', who denounces the very 'brutality' that he himself 'creates, perpetuates and exploits, and which he moreover baptises "freedom of labour"'.[19]

Marx utilised the reports of government and Privy Council inspectors and commissioners extensively to illustrate the conditions of industrial capitalist exploitation in England, Wales and Scotland. They paint a grim picture of life in the mines, mills and factories of mid-19th century Britain for the new industrial working class, who worked long hours — often 12 or 16 a day and longer — six days a week. Marx was acutely aware of the ways in which women and child workers were exploited more intensively than many of their male counterparts, used to pull or drive down wages and labour standards, all with the aim of maximising profit. His coverage of this aspect of capitalist production has until recently received very little attention in otherwise admirable presentations and discussions of *Capital*.

In Volumes I and III, Marx highlighted the plight of numerous categories of women workers, usually bracketed with children which reflected their similar status in law and the battles fought between factory reformers and ruthless employers. He recalled the employment in the coal mines, alongside men, of naked women and children because they were cheaper than machines. Only after this was outlawed in 1842 did the coalowners introduce substantially more machinery. Until then, Marx remarked sarcastically, this policy had been sanctioned by the capitalists' moral code 'and especially by their ledgers'. In England, too, women were still used to haul canal boats, because they were cheaper than machines and horses: 'Hence nowhere do we find a more shameful squandering of human labour power for the most despicable purposes than in England, the land of machinery'.[20]

Reporting on London's dressmakers, milliners and seamstresses, he cites a London physician who wrote of their 'three miseries — overwork, deficient air, and either deficient food or deficient digestion'. Marx retails the case of 20-year old Mary Anne Walkley, who had worked with 60 other young women (30 in one room) for 261/2 hours without a break, kept going on sherry, port and coffee, slept on the premises and then dropped dead. A doctor told the inquest that she had died from 'long hours of work in an over-crowded workroom, and a too small and badly ventilated bedroom'. The female proprietor of what was reputedly one of the finest millinery establishments in London had been shocked ... by Walkley's failure to complete her assignment.[21]

Marx cited the reports of the Children's Employment Commission, one of which exposed the night-time work of young girls and women on the pit banks and coke heaps of south Wales and Staffordshire. Whether the women ('begrimed with dirt and smoke') shared the same sensibilities about the 'unfeminine' character of their work, dress and behaviour as the commissioners is moot. Marx quoted such judgements without comment, while clearly deploring the conditions in which many women and children were employed. These including night-time labour with its 'generally injurious influence', not least in the paper-making industry where employers could easily breach the 12-hour limit (10 hours in textile mills) on young and female labour required by law.[22] In the face of further restrictions, many manufacturers dismissed a substantial number of their young and women employees, worked the men for longer and found loopholes to keep children alongside them in what Marx called a 'pro-slavery rebellion'.[23] This even included the employers' fight against the 1845 Print Works' Act which limited daily hours for women in the printing industry to 16, banning night work but with no compulsory pause for meal breaks (and which Marx characterised as a 'Parliamentary abortion').[24] He followed in detail the long struggle over factory legislation as it affected both male and female workers, with detailed attention to women and children, mocking the Christian and patriotic pretensions of innumerable cruel and dishonest capitalists.

Capital also reproduces masses of evidence from official reports of the impact of the new factory system on the health and physiology of many industrial workers, but especially upon women and children. High death rates among the latter groups were, he insisted against complacent champions of the Factory Acts (which applied only to the cotton and most other textile industries), 'principally due to the employment of the mothers away from their homes, and to the neglect and maltreatment, consequent on her absence, such as, amongst others, insufficient nourishment, unsuitable food, and dosing with opiates; besides this, there arises an unnatural estrangement between mother and child, and as a consequence intentional starving and poisoning of the children'. He contrasted this state of affairs in the industrial districts with that in the many rural areas where agriculture employed far fewer women.[25]

One result of the extraordinary productiveness of modern industry, Marx noted, was the availability of an ever larger part of the working class for unproductive employment in domestic service. This represented the 'consequent reproduction, on a constantly extending scale, of the ancient domestic slaves under the name of a servant class'. According to the 1861 census in England and Wales, the total number had grown over the preceding decade by 18% to 1.2m — about the same as in the mines and textile factories combined and a little more than in the textile and metal industries together: 'What a splendid result of the capitalist exploitation of machinery!', Marx exclaimed. He subsequently noted (and overestimated) the increase in the number of male servants over the following decade to 1871, and that 'the young servant girls in the houses of the London lower middle class are in common parlance called "slaveys"'.[26] But nowhere does he mention the fact that 89% of all domestic servants were females and that these comprised 33% of all female workers (while only 2% of male workers were in domestic service).[27]

Capitalism had also set in motion another army of labour — the domestic or homeworkers, carrying out contract work in houses, garrets and workrooms. This putting-out system exploits 'cheap and immature labour power' all the more shamelessly, pitting the homeworker against factory machinery or skilled labour in remaining workshops. They were preyed upon by 'plundering parasites' and had neither the power of resistance of a large workforce nor any protection against gross overwork (for example, in the lace finishing and straw-plaiting industries) and the toxic substances to be found in the metal, printing, bookbinding, candle-making, rag-sorting and other trades.[28] Marx inveighed against wretched exploitation and poverty of young female workers, quoting from reports of the ignorance, vice and illegitimacy that abounded among a population whose 'morality is at the lowest ebb'.[29] Finally, there is an end to this 'cheapening of labour power, by sheer abuse of the labour of women and children, by sheer robbery of every normal condition requisite for working and living, and by the sheer brutality of overwork and night-work'. Factories spring up and the female workers, notably in clothing manufacture, are compelled to enter them and work their new machinery.[30] The new machine hands are girls and young women, whose overworked energy and flexibility drive out the older men and younger children.

Whereas the 1866 Children's Employment Commission report condemned parents for abusing their authority and turning their children into wage-earning machines, Marx declared that 'on the contrary, it was the capitalistic mode of exploitation which, by sweeping away the economic basis of parental authority, made its exercise degenerate into a mischievous misuse of power'. He added:

> However terrible and disgusting the dissolution, under the capitalist system, of the old family ties may appear, nevertheless, modern industry, by assigning as it does an important part in the process of production, outside the domestic sphere, to women, to young persons, and to children of both sexes, creates a new economic foundation for a higher form of the family and of the relations between the sexes.

Here, for Marx, was the potential for an historic advance for women.

> The fact of the collective working group being composed of individuals of both sexes and all ages, must necessarily, under suitable conditions, become a source of humane development; although in its spontaneously developed, brutal, capitalistic form, where the labourer exists for the process of production, and not the process of production for the labourer, that fact is a pestiferous source of corruption and slavery.[31]

Such conditions would include the 1867 legislation extending the maximum 10-hour day for women and children to the rest of the textile industries and to almost all other factories and mills employing 50 workers or more (one of the 'vicious exceptions' and 'cowardly compromises with the masters' lambasted by Marx). Thus he told the General Council of the IWMA in July 1868: 'This was a step of progress, in so far as it afforded more leisure time to the work-people'. The rise of the machine had forced women and children into the factory, he remarked:

> The woman has thus become an active agent in our social production. Formerly female and children's labour was carried on within the family circle. I do not say that it is wrong that women and children should participate in our social production. I think every child above the age of nine ought to be employed at productive labour a portion of its time, but the way in which they are made to work under existing circumstances is abominable.[32]

Whereas Marx believed that women's employment tended to be more intensively exploited than men's, his response in *Capital* was not to propose 'equal pay for women', at least for work of equal value. This had yet to become a familiar slogan or demand in the working class movement anywhere in Western Europe. It had been raised by women and their male supporters in the Owenite movement in the 1830s, including its Grand National Consolidated Trade Union for unskilled and general workers. However, the unions for skilled male workers preferred to bar the entry of women into their trade, or to restrict the work they could perform, while demanding a 'breadwinner's wage' for the male worker with a family back at home. Other causes received priority, notably trade union rights, the electoral franchise, shorter hours and factory reform. Only after many more women had formed or joined trade unions did the Trades Union Congress agree a resolution in 1888 in favour of equal pay for women doing the same work as men.

Before then, Marx had accepted an invitation to draft a preamble to the electoral programme of the French Workers' Party in 1881. He and Engels also helped draw up its minimum programme, which supported 'equal wages for workers of both sexes'.[33] Some years later, after Marx's death, Engels confirmed his view that 'equal wages for equal work regardless of sex are, so far as I know, demanded by all socialists until such time as wages are totally abolished'. However, he also believed that the working woman's 'special physiological functions' required special protection against capitalist exploitation; hence he rejected the demand of some English female campaigners for the removal of all restrictions on women's work (for example, working underground in the coal industry) which, he said, amounted to 'women's formal right to allow themselves to be as thoroughly exploited by capitalists as men are'. For himself, he told his correspondent:

> I must confess that I am more interested in the health of the coming generation than in absolute, formal equality between the sexes during the final years of the capitalist mode of production. True equality between men and women can, or so I am convinced, become a reality only when the exploitation of both by capital has been abolished, and private work in the home been transformed into a public industry.[34]

The capitalist world may be a little closer to formal equality between the sexes today than 100 years and more ago. True equality remains a lot further away. Globally, women's participation in the labour market remains at a substantially lower rate (49%) than that for men (76%), although the participation rate for both has been falling over the past 20 years since 1997. The gap is even bigger in the developing countries, especially in North Africa, the Middle East and Southern Asia.[35] Western Europe is one of the few regions where the gap is expected to continue narrowing, as more women enter the labour market while men leave it.

The differential in unemployment rates is not so large, with the highest jobless levels — more than 20% — persisting in North Africa and the Middle East. Women tend to work longer hours, at home as well as in work (the 'double shift'), while those who would prefer full-time work to part-time are less likely than men to have it. There is also significant gender segregation in employment, with women more concentrated in education, health and social care; in the lower paid service and retail sectors; in clerical support in the developed countries; and in agriculture, forestry and fisheries in the developing countries.

Gender segregation is a major factor behind the gender pay gap which still exists in almost every country, while pay inequality between male and female workers doing work of equal value continues to be a significant cause in some developing economies. Even so, women having paid employment appears to be a major factor in lifting households out of poverty, notably in Latin America, the Caribbean and the Middle East. Since the revolutionary Soviet government decreed equal treatment for women workers, maternity rights and equal pay for equal work in 1918, many Communist and social-democratic governments have since followed suit in the socialist and developed capitalist countries, in the latter case usually after periods of mass agitation by trade union and women's organisations.

In Britain, the Annual Survey of Pay and Earnings estimated the median gross hourly earnings for men to be 10% higher than for women in 2017. Full-time women earn less than men in every occupational group and regardless of age or length of service; part-time workers likewise, except for young and middle-aged women and among workers with less than five years' service. While occupational and working patterns explain some of the difference, the Office for National Statistics is at a loss to account for 64% of it.[36]

Internationally, many of the gender inequalities reflect deep and oppressive social and cultural traditions, standards and attitudes which facilitate additional exploitation in the workplace. The response, therefore, has to be an ideological as well as an economic and political one. Trade unionism has played a central role in organising women at work and campaigning against the worst injustices, although only when unions take account of the need to conduct their recruitment, organisational, collective bargaining and mobilising activities accordingly. Equal pay for work of equal value, maternity rights, rights for domestic service workers, forced labour, child exploitation and violence and sexual harassment in the workplace remain key issues, along with the extra dangers facing female migrant workers ensnared in trafficking.

Yet trade unionism among women workers — and among men — remains at a low level in most countries. More positively, the gap between the sexes in terms of trade union density has narrowed or even been reversed in many countries. While a lower proportion of the female labour force is unionised in, for example, the USA (10%), Spain (15%), Netherlands (17%), Japan (13%), Germany, Austria, Belgium, Cyprus, Bulgaria and Slovakia, it remains higher among women in Sweden (74%) and the other Scandinavian countries, Ireland (32%), Hungary (13%), the Baltic states, Poland and Slovenia.[37]

In Britain, due in part to their concentration in the public sector, more women workers are unionised (26% in 2017) than men (21%), in full-time and in part-time employment. Both shares are lower than 20 years before. In fact, women have comprised the majority (54% in 2017) of trade union members in Britain since 2005. Some 28% of working women are covered by collective bargaining arrangements, but only 24% of men. The average hourly earnings of women trade unionists are 22% higher than those of non-unionised women workers.[38]

National and international trade union organisations, often in alliance with the with other campaigning bodies and the International Labour Organisation (ILO), are exposing and challenging the super-exploitation of women and child labour by transnational corporations (TNCs) in their supply chains. National government and trade union action is needed in the major imperialist countries to enforce ILO conventions and penalise those TNCs that breach them.

In the most developed economies, equal opportunities in training and promotion are higher on the agenda. Women workers everywhere also benefit disproportionately from gains in areas where male workers directly benefit, too, such as securing statutory minimum wages, job security, social welfare protection, adequate retirement pensions and coverage by collective bargaining arrangements.

The role that women's work in the home often plays in replenishing male labour power — as identified by Marx in *Capital* — has prompted 'wages for housework' initiatives in the USA, Britain and other advanced capitalist countries. In most Marxist and trade union circles, however, this has been regarded as more of a diversionary or divisive demand, detracting from the emphasis that should be placed on united struggles for equal pay at work and higher wages for all (including the 'social wage' for single parents and unemployed workers).

'Estrangement' (or alienation)

In Volume I of *Capital*, Marx provided detailed an historical and contemporary account of the class struggle in England, Scotland and Wales over surplus value. Battles were fought over the length of the working day, night work, work systems and women's and child labour throughout the period from England's 14th century Labour Statutes to Britain's 19th century Factory Acts. In particular, his accounts of the rise and impact of machinery and the factory system draw from a host of sources relating to England, Scotland, Wales and continental Europe. Referring to the machine as the 'material embodiment of capital', he returned to an earlier theme about the dehumanising effect ('estrangement') of mechanisation and automation on the labour process, on the machine operative and on those handicraft workers who lose their livelihoods as their skills are rendered redundant.[39]

In the 1857-58 *Economic Manuscripts*, he had argued that the development of society's productive forces had enshrined ('reified') past labour in the huge machinery that dominates living labour — indeed, to the point that it appears (at least to the capitalist) that the machine is independent of the worker. Society's labour has set up an 'enormous objectified power' which it sees as an alienated force over and against itself, and which belongs to capital.[40] That machinery should appear so to the capitalist and the worker is an historical necessity as part of capitalist development.

Yet this is merely one aspect of capitalism's appropriation of living labour and, in effect, 'alienating' it from itself, objectifying it whether in the form of machinery or as the commodities produced by living labour and then removed from it.

Technology and the division (specialisation) of labour have further transformed the labour process and workplaces in the course of the 20th century, particularly in the advanced capitalist economies. Many workers still feel alienated from their work, the workplace and its modern machinery. Numerous studies published by bodies from the Trades Union Congress (TUC) in Britain to the ILO in Geneva describe and explain how the introduction of the most modern technology — computerisation, automation, etc. — and the pressures of globalised competition have greatly increased workplace stress.[41]

As Marx had put it in his *Economic and Philosophic Manuscripts of 1844*:

> Labour is external to the worker ... in his work, therefore, he does not affirm himself but denies himself, does not feel content but unhappy, does not develop freely his physical and mental energy but mortifies his body and ruins his mind. The worker therefore only feels himself outside his work, and in his work feels outside himself. He feels at home when he is not working, and when he is working he does not feel at home. His labour is therefore not voluntary, but coerced; it is forced labour. It is therefore not the satisfaction of a need; it is merely a means to satisfy needs external to it. Its alien character emerges clearly in the fact that as soon as no physical or other compulsion exists, labour is shunned like the plague.[42]

Cyclical crises

The 1857-58 Manuscripts elaborate Marx's theory of economic crisis. A portion of surplus value is re-invested as wage-capital (approximating to v), exploits labour and emerges afresh as expanded value (s) seeking further profitable investment. This process of expanded reproduction accelerates into a boom.

But capitalism's recurring problem is that while the capitalist class constantly seeks to maximise profit, not least by exerting downward pressure on wages, this accumulation of capital outstrips the capacity of the working class to buy all that its labour power produces at a profitable price for the capitalists. Capital accumulates which cannot find a profitable outlet and, as a consequence, engages in ever more speculative ventures. More is being produced that can be sold at a profit. The result is that products go unsold or have to be offloaded at a loss. Companies cut back their production and investment plans. Some go out of business. Workers are laid off, reducing purchasing power in the economy still further. Production and investment go into a downward spiral. Economic slowdown turns into recession and, in the most severe cases, slump. Only when labour power and the means of production are cheap enough to return a profit do production and then investment begin to recover as the cycle begins once more.

As Marx summarised this cycle in Volume I of *Capital* itself:

The enormous power, inherent in the factory system, of expanding by jumps, and the dependence of that system on the markets of the world, necessarily beget feverish production, followed by overfilling of the markets, whereupon contraction of the markets brings on crippling of production. The life of modern industry becomes a series of periods of moderate activity, prosperity, overproduction, crisis and stagnation.[43]

This is the cyclical character of capitalism's crises of generalised overproduction, which the orthodox economists in Marx's day made 'childish' attempts to deny.[44] Since then, cyclical crises have been a recurring feature of established, developed capitalist economies. Britain, for instance, has experienced the depressions of 1919-21 and 1930-31 and the recessions of 1952, 1958, 1974-75, 1980-81, 1991 and 2008-09, when aggregate GDP still fell, though not as severely. In the US, by far the world's biggest economy throughout the post-war period, GDP dropped in 1954, 1958, 1974-75, 1982, 1991, 2001 and 2008-09. Most Western European economies, including Germany and France, shared the recessions of the mid-1970s, early 1990s, 2001-02 and 2008-09, less so in the early 1980s, and the growing international synchronisation of the most advanced capitalist economies is clear.[45]

While these crises all had their own particular characteristics, they also exhibited the common features of over-accumulation and over-production to a greater or lesser degree. In addition, especially during the post-war expansion between 1945 and 1973, there were cyclical slowdowns in economic growth that did not dip into recession and an absolute decline in national economic output.

Of course, capitalism's tame economists deny that these crises arise as the result of contradictions within the capitalist mode of production related to over-accumulation and over-production. They prefer to identify 'business cycles' that merely describe a crisis. Explanations are rare and very unconvincing, usually attributing turbulence to insufficient demand or — because of various factors — insufficient supply. Capitalism's apologists also tend to exaggerate the uncommon features of each crisis (such as world oil price rises in 1973-74) in order to separate each crisis from the others, denying or downplaying their common features, thereby concealing their origin in capitalism's own systemic contradictions.

Within the Marxist tradition in the 20th century, Dutch economists Jacob van Gelderen and Salomon de Wolff and, later, Soviet economist Nikolai Kondratiev claimed to detect long waves of economic growth and slowdown in the course of capitalist development internationally. These cover periods of 45-60 years at a time, encompass over-production cycles and are linked by most Marxist proponents of the theory to technological innovations such as the steam engine, iron smelting and the railways, engineering, motor vehicles and oil and, most recently, information technology. Non-Marxist 'long wave' theories emphasise the role of demographic change, land speculation or levels of credit and debt.

Capital accumulation and the 'reserve army'

Part VII of *Capital* Volume I contained much new and ground-breaking material on the 'Accumulation of Capital'. A portion of surplus value is converted into capital for expansion, divided between extra investment in both labour power (v) and in means of production (c). But the onward march of technology, mechanisation and labour productivity means that the amount of c in the economy as a whole grows faster than the amount of v. Even though extra labour will be employed actually producing the means of production (machines, tools, energy, etc.), this will be counteracted by the spread of labour-saving technology. Furthermore and in any event, there will usually be limits on the speed and extent to which the labour force can expand through procreation or immigration.

One effect of the accumulation of capital, Marx noted, is that the amount of capital owned by the individual capitalist or association of capitalists grows in a process he calls 'concentration'. But the intensified competition for surplus value also gives rise to a process of 'centralisation': the 'expropriation of capitalist by capitalist' and the 'transformation of many small into few larger capitals'.[46]

Volume II of *Capital* highlighted the importance of the timescale in which a given portion of capital circulates and expands. The faster the turnover, the quicker the accumulation and the bigger the mass of profit over a particular period of time. The credit system, which develops along with capitalism generally, accelerates both production and consumption as well as facilitating the concentration of capital.

The increased demand for labour power that accompanies capital accumulation, as both c and v grow in absolute terms, compounds the displacement of labour in particular industries. As Marx put it in Volume I: 'The whole form of the movement of modern industry depends, therefore, upon the constant transformation of a part of the labouring population into unemployed or half-employed hands'.[47] Workers employed in agriculture and textiles were early casualties of technological advance, and he wrote movingly in *Capital* about their plight.[48] As a consequence, where sections of a multiplying population are relatively surplus to requirements, a more or less permanent 'disposable industrial reserve army' of labour is formed, which can be recruited for work during a boom and quickly expelled during recession and slump.[49] Moreover, its very existence is essential to capital accumulation, because it exerts pressure on employed workers to submit to greater exploitation — through productivity measures or wage restraint — for fear of losing their job to reservists waiting in the wings.

During the long economic expansion from the end of the Second World War until 1970, Britain's unemployment rate did not fall below the 'full employment' rate of 3% as defined by William Beveridge. Post-war Labour and Tory governments pursued the objective of 'full and stable employment' first set out in the Economic Policy White Paper published in May 1944. Governments in the USA, Australia and elsewhere quickly followed suit. Since 1980, the unemployment rate in the G7 group of leading capitalist countries has not fallen more than fractionally below 5%. In fact, it has gone through four dramatic cycles over that time, reaching peaks of 81/2%. Historically, after the freak period brought on by world war and the destruction of value on an epic scale, capitalism has returned to normal — complete with its reserve army of labour, its serried ranks of migrant workers and all those others conscripted into temporary, casual, flexible and zero-hour contract work.

'Primitive accumulation'

The final Part VIII of *Capital* Volume I constitutes the most searing indictment of the methods by which capitalism established itself. Outlining the 'So-Called Primitive Accumulation' of capital, Marx recounted in fine detail the depredations inflicted on the agricultural populations of Wales, Scotland, the English counties and Ireland from the late 16th century onwards, ruthlessly sweeping away small peasant producers and culminating in the Highland Clearances. They were separated from the means of production (land, small-scale machinery and tools) and turned into urban or rural labourers now 'free' to sell their labour power, as some landowners and emergent capitalist farmers stole common land and turned to large-scale mechanised commodity production. Obversely, the primitive accumulation of capital also produced and necessitated a primitive accumulation of labour power.

Several chapters detail the harsh and cruel legislation enacted against those who had been expropriated — liberated from their previous livelihoods — whipping and mutilating them for vagrancy and vagabondage, press-ganging the unemployed and destitute into military service, extending the working day, limiting wages, outlawing strikes and workers' combinations. Marx drew parallels with similar measures in France and Germany.

In Chapter XXX (30) on the 'Genesis of the Industrial Capitalist', he laid bare the brutal means by which money was accumulated for use as industrial capital (as c and v). The dissolution of feudalism, with its expropriation and clearance of the rural population, made possible the transformation of money made from trade and credit. Marx summarised the other main sources thus:

> The discovery of gold and silver in America, the extirpation, enslavement and entombment in mines of the aboriginal population, the beginning of the conquest and looting of the East Indies, the turning of Africa into a warren for the commercial hunting of blackskins, signalised the rosy dawn of the era of capitalist production. These idyllic proceedings are the chief momenta of primitive accumulation. On their heels treads the commercial war of the European nations, with the globe for a theatre. It begins with the revolt of the Netherlands from Spain, assumes giant dimension in England's Anti-Jacobin War, and is still going on in the opium wars against China, &c.[50]

Chapter XXX of Volume I goes on to highlight the role of state power in organising colonial trade monopolies, the National Debt, taxation and trade protectionism to accelerate the transformation of the feudal mode of production into the capitalist mode in Spain, Portugal, Holland, France and — from the late 17th century — England. He reserved special scorn for the way in which Christian colonists, with the backing of governments and parliaments in the 'mother country', enslaved or massacred native peoples from Indonesia and Africa to the West Indies, Mexico and the United States. Due prominence is given to the role of the nexus linking the slave trade, shipping, colonial plantation, the cotton industry and child labour in the take-off of British capitalism: 'the veiled slavery of the wage workers in Europe needed, for its pedestal, slavery pure and simple in the new world'.[51]

While primitive accumulation had been more or less completed in Western Europe, capitalism still had to expropriate the many independent producers in Europe's colonial settlements. Otherwise, there could be no supply of labour for commodity production there, no development of labour's enormous productive power on the basis of large-scale machinery, cooperation and division of tasks. In the USA and Canada, for instance, this failure to divorce colonists from the means of production — especially the land — had retarded the development of industry and its necessary separation from agriculture. In the American case, mass immigration, civil war and with it the raising of a National Debt and taxes, together with the huge allocation of public land to mining, railway construction, etc. had spurred the rapid development of capitalist production. A similar path had also been taken in Australia.

Unsurprisingly, much of this account of primitive accumulation differs radically from the those in numerous Western history and economics textbooks over the past 150 years and even today. Many pro-capitalist historians and economists simply equate the onset of capitalism with the expansion of domestic and international trade and then industrialisation. The initial finance is attributed to thrift, royal patronage, family collectivism, merchant profit, commercial credit and overseas discoveries, allowing barely a minor role to the slave trade and slavery.

In reality, according to Marx, the capitalist mode of production transforms the mass of the population into wage labourers and their means of production into capital, which itself comes into the world 'dripping from head to foot, from every pore, with blood and dirt'.[52]

Historical parallels can be misleading, if not wholly misconceived and erroneous. Yet they can be detected in the huge shifts in population from the countryside to industrial areas, towns and cities that have taken place in many parts of the Third World, as part of a process of primitive accumulation. In some countries, notably India, this has been driven by landowning and industrial capitalist interests and facilitated by legislation. But in the biggest example of all, China, parallels have been contradicted because the process has been centrally planned by a socialist state in order to develop what the Chinese Communist Party calls the 'primary stage' of socialism. Unlike early industrial capitalism in Britain and elsewhere, China is implementing policies to provide social protection for urban workers and to stimulate economic development in rural areas.

Concentration, centralisation, globalisation

In Chapter XXXII (32) of Volume I, Marx indicated how capitalism's primitive accumulation necessarily dissolves private, self-earned property in the means of production based on the labour of its owner. This is the case whether that property is the land of the peasant or the tool of the artisan. Such a pattern of small-scale production, which had survived ancient slave-society and feudalism, was incompatible with capitalism's concentration of the means of production to create a vast socially integrated mode of production based on cooperation, a division of labour and control and application of the forces of nature.

In 'annihilating' — Marx's term — the old order, capitalism transformed the scattered and individualised means of production of the many into the huge property of the few. As the smallholders and artisans are expropriated and turned into propertyless labourers ('proletarians') to be employed and exploited so, in turn, are many small capitalists driven out by bigger: 'one capitalist kills many'.[53] This centralisation is an essential feature of a system that expands to create a world market which entangles all peoples in its net.

The 20th century witnessed an enormous acceleration in these processes of concentration and centralisation and the extension of a capitalist world market.

Marx laid bare the forces and tendencies that shaped modern capitalism. But he could not have anticipated the precise forms, relations and mechanisms that would characterise such development. Only after his death did Karl Kautsky and VI Lenin propose the theory that capitalism had entered a qualitatively new stage, namely, 'imperialism'. Economically, in the biggest and most advanced capitalist societies (Britain, France, the USA and Germany), free competition had turned into its opposite, namely, monopoly. Through growth, merger and takeover accelerated by periodic crises, a small number of companies had come to monopolise most sectors of the economy.

In his classic work, *Imperialism: the Highest Stage of Capitalism* (1916), Lenin identified the other defining economic features of capitalism in its imperialist stage: banking capital fusing with industrial capital to create finance capital controlled by a financial oligarchy; the export of capital — as distinct from goods — assuming exceptional significance; the formation of 'international monopolist capitalist associations' sharing the world between them; and the biggest capitalist powers dividing up the world between each other.[54] In these conditions, monopolies in the imperialist heartlands could export surplus capital to reap super-profits from the super-exploitation of non-unionised, cheap and 'flexible' labour to obtain raw materials in the colonies and semi-colonies.

This last feature would not have been unknown to Marx, even though it did not achieve such prominence until after his death. In Volume III of *Capital*, he noted that 'if capital is sent abroad, this is not done because it absolutely could not be applied at home, but because it can be employed at a higher rate of profit in a foreign country'.[55] This and other features of imperialism identified by Lenin are, obviously, more pronounced in some developed capitalist countries than in others. Nonetheless, the drive to monopoly is common to all, as is the spread of their monopoly corporations across the world.

By 2018, of the world's biggest 150 economic entities by Gross Domestic Product (in the case of countries) or revenue (for companies), the top 24 were countries, headed by the USA, China, Japan, Germany, Britain, France, India, Italy, Brazil and Canada.[56] Monopoly corporations made up almost two-thirds of the others and more than half of the total.[57] Most of the names will be familiar: Walmart, Royal Dutch Shell, Volkswagen, Toyota Motor, BP, Apple, ExxonMobil, BP, Samsung, Daimler. Each of the first three has a turnover bigger than the GDP of at least 150 — more than three-quarters — of the world's countries. The scale of Royal Dutch Shell's operations is bigger than Portugal's entire economy. Oil and other energy corporations comprise the biggest group, with vehicles, electronics and IT, banking and retail corporations following closely behind. Thanks mainly to China, a growing number of the top corporations are state-owned, notably in energy, banking and construction.

Most significantly, the world's biggest companies as measured across a range of indicators — assets, market value and profits as well as sales — are banks and other financial institutions. They comprise nine of the top ten in the 2018 Forbes Global 2000 list.

As most of these giant companies are TNCs, carrying out their operations in more than one country, they straddle the international economy. They have helped to form and intensify a world market in which the processes of production, trade and commerce are increasingly integrated internationally. At the same time, it should be emphasised that all but a handful of TNCs have a home country whose national state power is usually exercised in their interests. In 2018, according to the Forbes 2000 rankings, most of the biggest 100 are based in the USA (30), with others in mainland China (17), Japan (8), Germany (8), Britain (5), Switzerland (4) and the Russian Federation (4):

The world's biggest 100 companies, 2018 ($bn)

Company Top 1-10	Country	Sales	Profits	Assets	Market Value
Ind. & Comm. Bank*	China	165	44	4,211	311
China Constrn. Bank*	China	143	37	3,632	261
JP Morgan Chase	USA	118	27	2,610	388
Berkshire Hathaway	USA	235	40	703	492
Agricul. Bank of China*	China	129	30	3,439	184
Bank of America	USA	103	20	2,329	314
Wells Fargo	USA	102	22	1,915	265
Apple	USA	248	53	368	927
Bank of China*	China	118	26	3,204	159
Ping An Insurance*	China	142	14	1,066	181

Top 11-20

Royal Dutch Shell	Netherlands	322	15	411	307
Toyota Motor	Japan	265	23	473	201
ExxonMobil	USA	230	20	349	344
Samsung Electronics	Sth Korea	225	41	293	326
AT&T	USA	159	31	446	198
Volkswagen Group	Germany	272	13	531	101
HSBC Holdings	Britain	63	11	2,652	200
Verizon Comms.	USA	128	31	265	201
BNP Paribas	France	118	9	2,354	94
Microsoft	USA	103	14	246	751

Top 21-30

Chevron	USA	139	10	256	248
Allianz	Germany	123	8	1,129	100
Alphabet	USA	118	17	207	766
Walmart	USA	500	10	205	246
China Mobile	Hong Kong	110	17	234	193
Total	France	156	8	257	168
Sinopec*	China	327	8	250	139
United Health Group	USA	208	11	156	229
Daimler	Germany	193	12	323	86
PetroChina**	China	282	4	381	220

Top 31-40

Banco Santander	Spain	56	8	1,769	106
China Merchants Bank	China	50	11	994	112
AXA Group	France	150	7	1,029	64
Comcast	USA	87	23	191	147
China Life Insurance*	China	97	6	474	104
BP	Britain	252	4	275	153
Mitsubishi UFJ Financl.	Japan	52	9	2,774	86
Bank of Comms.*	China	59	11	1,473	67
Softbank	Japan	83	9	293	85
BMW Group	Germany	114	10	41	2

Top 41-50

Anheuser-Busch InBev	Belgium	56	8	249	184
Royal Bank of Canada	Canada	41	9	1,040	113
Gazprom**	Russia	112	12	317	58
Pfizer	USA	53	22	165	208
Itaú Unibanco Holding	Brazil	62	8	438	87
Nippon T'graph & Tel	Japan	105	8	191	96
Sberbank*	Russia	46	13	471	86
Nestle	Switzerland	91	7	134	237

| Intel | USA | 64 | 11 | 129 | 255 |
| Morgan Stanley | USA | 46 | 7 | 858 | 98 |

Top 51-60

Siemens	Germany	95	7	163	113
Boeing	USA	96	9	114	200
Amazon.com	USA	193	4	126	778
TD Bank Group	Canada	36	8	1,028	108
Procter & Gamble	USA	66	10	124	185
ING Group	Netherlands	57	6	1,016	62
Postal Savings Bank*	China	56	8	1,467	55
Honda Motor	Japan	139	10	182	59
Sumitomo Mitsui Fin.	Japan	49	7	1,848	58
Goldman Sachs Group	USA	44	5	974	92

Top 61-70

Intesa Sanpaolo	Italy	43	8	957	63
Industrial Bank**	China	48	9	1,023	54
Novartis	Switzerland	50	8	136	203
Glencore International	Switzerland	205	6	136	76
Banco Bradesco	Brazil	77	5	371	62
Prudential	Britain	112	3	655	68
Ford Motor	USA	160	8	267	45
IBM	USA	81	6	125	132
CVS Health	USA	186	7	135	66
Shanghai PD Bank**	China	48	8	975	51

Top 71-80

Commonwealth Bank	Australia	33	8	752	94
Walt Disney	USA	59	12	98	152
Prudential Financial	USA	61	8	830	42
Rosneft**	Russia	95	4	214	69
Enel	Italy	87	5	194	62
Citic Pacific**	Hong Kong	58	6	962	44
Facebook	USA	45	18	89	542
MetLife	USA	64	4	713	48
Deutsche Telekom	Germany	85	4	179	81
SAIC Motor*	China	137	5	118	64

Top 81-90

Alibaba	China	38	10	114	499
BASF	Germany	75	7	99	95
Reliance Industries	India	61	6	125	93
State Constructn. Eng.*	China	162	5	258	40
China Citic Bank*	China	44	7	894	47

Sony	Japan	77	4	179	60
Westpac Banking	Australia	29	6	669	76
Bank of Nova Scotia	Canada	29	7	753	75
Brit. American Tobacco	Britain	26	48	191	120
Minsheng Banking	China	43	7	954	44

Top 91-100

Equinor*	Norway	65	5	115	90
AIA Group	Hong Kong	32	6	213	111
Roche Holding	Switzerland	54	9	79	190
Lloyds Banking Group	Britain	34	4	1,099	65
Eni**	Italy	76	4	143	71
Charter Comms.	USA	42	10	146	65
Nissan Motor	Japan	107	7	174	40
LukOil	Russia	100	7	92	61
United Technologies	USA	61	5	99	100
Bayer	Germany	44	8	93	105

* mostly or wholly in public ownership
** mixed ownership but under state control

In the domestic economies of the main capitalist countries, monopoly domination is almost total.

In Britain, for example, the revenue share of the biggest 100 companies across the economy as a whole rose steadily from 18.5% in 2004 to just over 25% by 2010. The after-shock of the Great Crash pushed it down towards 23% in 2016, but there is little reason not to believe that it will resume its upward trajectory.[58] The centralisation of capital has grown in most of the major sectors since 2003, including by 11% in manufacturing, so that the position is as follows according to the Department for Business, Energy & Industrial Strategy:[59]

Centralisation of monopoly capital in Britain (2015)

	Share of turnover in each sector (%)		Sectoral
	Top 5	Top 15	turnover (£bn)
Wholesale	40	50	837
Manufacturing	15	25	585
Banking	50	80	579
Retailing	30	45	386
Other financial services	50	80	144
Insurance	55	85	114
Road transport	35	50	98
Electricity distribution	85	100	66
Telecoms	60	75	60
Air transport	55	70	39
Oil & gas extraction	40	70	38

Broadcasting media	25	40	24
Electricity generation & trade	n/a*	75	22
Postal services	60	75	21
Programming & broadcasting	n/a**	90	15
Rail transport	55	90	13
Information services	50	65	13
Water services	60	95	10
Gas distribution	85	100	5
Mining & quarrying	50	70	5
Software & games	45	65	2

* The top 10 have 65%.
** The top 10 have 85% and in 2011 the top 5 had 70%.

While the degree of centralisation in the manufacturing sector is not so pronounced, this is not the case in a number of its sub-sectors here as well as elsewhere. For example, as calculated by Bell & Tomlinson (2018), the share of sales revenue captured by the top 5 corporations in various sub-sectors is as follows: vehicle manufacture (78%), iron and steel making (86%), agrochemicals (77%), beer brewing, (88%) sugar processing (76%), oil refining (94%) chocolate confectionery (94%), open cast coalmining (88%), manufacture of domestic electrical appliances (52%) and newspaper publishing (60%).

As for concentration, in terms of market capitalisation (ie., the total shares value) at constant prices, the top 15 companies in 2006 were more than three times bigger than those in 1992. The same trends of centralisation and concentration occur in the USA, largely unhindered by the existence — as in Britain — of anti-monopoly legislation.[60] The US President's Council of Economic Advisers has reported a significant growth of centralisation in ten of 13 high-level sectors of the US economy between 1997 and 2012, particularly in the retail, transportation and warehousing sectors.[61] Even so, the levels of monopolisation in comparable sectors dominated by private ownership — notably banking, insurance, wholesale, retail and transportation — are substantially higher in Britain than in the USA.

Gustavo Grullon and others (2016) not only confirm the trend to centralisation across much of US industry, they also show that the big monopoly corporations reap higher profit margins. Furman & Orszag (2018) expose the link between higher monopolisation, slower wage growth and rising inequality.[62]

In Britain as elsewhere, the capitalist monopolies set the norms in each sector as far as prices, pay and technological development are concerned. In turn, they are now integrated into an oligarchy centred upon the City of London's financial institutions and markets. This finance capital exerts a decisive influence over the economy as a whole through interlocking shares and directorships and through its role in determining interest and currency rates, commodity prices and the availability of credit and investment. Of the top 15 FTSE companies in 1992, none were banks, ten were manufacturers and three were oil and gas producers; by 2004, the respective figures were six, five and three.[63]

Lenin also set out how, politically, imperialism meant a growth in the political power of the state in the core metropolitan countries and its merger with the economic power of the giant corporations, syndicates, trusts and cartels to constitute 'state-monopoly capitalism'. The role of the capitalist class as a progressive, democratising force in history had come to an end, as Marx had recognised in his own lifetime. It also meant the domination of other, less developed countries and their human and natural resources by the imperialist countries, whether through direct colonial rule or indirect, semi-colonial pressure. Either way, it was domination based ultimately on the threat or use of military force. For Lenin, the struggle between the imperialist powers to redivide the world in favour of their own monopolies had culminated in the 1914-18 Great War. Marx might not have predicted this imperialist world war — although Engels did with astonishing prescience in 1887 as he was editing Volume III of *Capital* — but he would not have been too surprised by its occurrence.[64]

'Pauperisation' — absolute and relative

Above all, Marx was sure that capitalism with its innate tendencies of concentration and centralisation cannot expand indefinitely while escaping its own growing contradictions. Towards the end of Volume I, he concluded:

> Along with the constantly diminishing number of the magnates of capital, who usurp and monopolise all advantages of this process of transformation, grows the mass of misery, oppression, slavery, degradation, exploitation; but with this too grows the revolt of the working class, a class always increasing in numbers, and disciplined, united, organised by the very mechanism of the process of capitalist production itself. The monopoly of capital becomes a fetter upon the mode of production, which has sprung up and flourished along with, and under it. Centralisation of the means of production and socialisation of labour at last reach a point where they become incompatible with their capitalist integument. This integument is burst asunder. The knell of capitalist private property sounds. The expropriators are expropriated.[65]

This is a highly significant passage, not only because Marx anticipates — on the basis of capitalism's tendencies exposed and outlined in *Capital* — the onward march of monopoly and the growing resistance of an increasingly strong working class movement. Above all, it identifies the irreconcilable contradiction at the core of the capitalist mode of production. This is the limit imposed by private, corporate, monopoly ownership of the means of production on the further development of society's productive forces necessary to meet humanity's needs and desires. This is what will compel the working class to use its strength to break with capitalist exploitation.

This thesis of pauperisation or 'immiseration' has been challenged by capitalism's proponents and disowned by some of capitalism's opponents. They have argued as though Marx meant, literally, that 'the mass of misery, oppression, slavery, degradation, exploitation' would increase in absolute terms for all or most workers over subsequent decades or centuries. To the contrary, defenders of the immiseration perspective have argued either: (a) that Marx implied in *Capital* (or later) that pauperisation would be relative, ie., that any improvement in the conditions of the working class would be substantially outstripped by improvements for the capitalist class; or (b) that Marx was, indeed, literally correct and the conditions of the working class as a whole, on average, globally, will worsen in real terms over the long term, ie., that pauperisation would be absolute — especially when broader factors are taken into account such as insecurity, stress and depression, environmental surroundings and general well-being.

The 'relative' pauperisation thesis is supported by most if not all estimates of trends in global inequality since 1850. Bourguignon and Morrisson (2002) calculate that inequality in income and consumption among the world's population as a whole rose more or less continuously — except for a period in the 1950s — until the 1980s, since when it appears to have fallen.[66] However, within these trends, it is important to distinguish between inequality within groups of countries at a similar level of development, and inequality between groups of countries at different levels.

Within the advanced capitalist countries, for instance, inequality generally declined and then stayed more or less constant from the post-World War One period until the 1970s. Inequality between the imperialist countries and the developing countries rose sharply until the 1950s and the era of colonial liberation, raising global levels of inequality accordingly. As imperialism reasserted its economic domination, inequality resumed its upward trend until the end of the 1980s. Since then, the continuous growth of China, India and Brazil in particular — including through the 2007-09 recession — has reversed the growth of inequality both globally and between the developed and developing countries, but not within many countries, whatever their level of development.

In terms of health and life expectancy, levels rose across the world between 1800 and 1950, but much more for one-third of the global population than for most of the remainder, making the planet a far more unequal place over that period. Between 1950 and 2012, progress continued to be almost universal, with major advances in China, India, Brazil and other developing economies hugely reducing inequality among two-thirds of the world's inhabitants. However, around 12% of human beings (mostly in Africa) suffer significantly higher levels of ill-health and lower levels of life expectancy than the rest, while at the top end of the scale the same proportion (mostly in the advanced imperialist countries) are in a substantially better position. Child mortality rates in low-income countries are ten times higher than in high-income ones. Overall, much of the evidence suggests that in terms of health and life expectancy, the world in 2012 was less unequal than in 1950 but more unequal than in 1800.[67]

In Britain, income inequality among all but the richest section of the population fell gradually from early in the 19th century and more sharply in the 20th century until the late 1970s. Since then, it has been climbing back towards pre-World War One levels.[68] In particular, the top 10% of recipients who had seen their share of total income fall from 39% in 1919 to 28% in the 1970s, had recovered that proportion by the end of the 1990s.[69]

Today, the Office for National Statistics (ONS) estimates that the top 10% of households receive almost one-third of all employment-related income (including executive and managerial salaries), 28% of all income from personal pensions and investments (48% of the latter) and just over one-quarter (£313bn) of total gross pre-tax annual income. Significantly, for this one-tenth of households, income from capital (£42bn) comprises only 13% of their total pre-tax income, suggesting that only a very small proportion of the adult population — no more than 2% — is dependent on capitalist dividends, interest or rent as their main source of income.

According to official estimates, the adults in 70% of Britain's households, who make up the bulk of the broadly defined working class, receive just over one-third of employment-related income, more than three-quarters of state pensions and benefits and less than half of total gross pre-tax income:

UK % distribution of household income (2016/17) [70]

	Bottom 70%	Middle 20%)	Top 10%
Employment income a	37	32	31
Capital income b	42	30	28
State transfers c	84	12	4
Pre-tax income d	45	29	26
Post-tax income e	51	26	23

a salaries (including company directors and managers), wages and self-employment income
b non-state personal pensions, annuities and investment income
c state pensions, benefits and tax credits
d gross income, before any direct or indirect taxation
e after paying all direct and indirect taxes

Based on previous research and estate duty records, Thomas Piketty (2014) estimates that the richest 10% of the population in Britain owned just over 80% of the wealth in 1810, rising to more than 90% over the following 100 years before falling steadily to around 63% by the end of the 1970s. Since then, that share has gone back up to 70%.[71] The most recent figures from the ONS claim that this same section of the population — which corresponds very roughly to the main owners of capital — possesses 'only' 44% (£5,595bn) of the total wealth in Britain in 2014-16, the same as in 2006-08. Clearly, this percentage is a gross underestimate, based as it is on a self-evaluation survey involving fewer than 0.1% of Britain's households and — despite various control checks — takes little account of unintentional under-assessment or dishonesty and concealment.[72] The same ONS survey would indicate that the poorest 70% of households own 24% of aggregate wealth:

Britain % distribution of household wealth (2014-16) [73]

	Bottom 70%	Middle 20%	Top 10%
Property wealth *a*	27	33	40
Financial wealth *b*	13	26	61
Private pension pot	20	34	46
All personal wealth *c*	24	32	44

a net of mortgage liability, excluding personal business property
b net of debt including overdrafts
c including other personal assets, net of debt, after taxation and excluding business assets

In reality, these official estimates grossly underestimate the unequal distribution of income and wealth in Britain today. A vast industry exists to hide the income and wealth of companies and rich individuals in order to minimise their tax liabilities, whether by legal or illegal means. In a report for the Public and Commercial Services (PCS) trade union, tax expert Richard Murphy calculated that annual rental revenue of around £3bn is not declared for income tax purposes (six times more than HMRC estimates); as many as 600,000 shareholders do not declare a total income from dividends of almost £6bn; while unreported capital gains income every year might amount to around £4bn. Murphy estimated very roughly that British residents had between £650bn and £950bn stashed illicitly in overseas tax havens in 2010.[74]

This scale of income and wealth concealment by the wealthy from Britain and elsewhere is confirmed in the millions of documents of the so-called Panama and Paradise Papers. Even the far smaller 'Swiss Leaks' files revealed that 8,844 British residents were holding $22bn (£14bn) in undisclosed bank accounts in just one branch (in Geneva) of one bank (HSBC) in one tax haven (Switzerland) in 2008.[75] Much of this income and wealth accrues to the richest 10% of the population. Its inclusion in the distribution figures would show even more pronounced patterns of income and wealth inequality in Britain.

According to Piketty (2014), the share of Britain's total national income going to capital (in the form of profits, dividends, interest and rent) has changed in inverse proportion to that of labour (including executive and managerial salaries) over the past 250 years. Capital's share rose as labour's fell in 1810-50, 1890-1910, 1920-40 and 1970-2000, while fortunes were reversed in the 1850-80s, 1910-20 and 1940-70 periods. In France, capital's share of national income fell from the First World War until the beginning of World War Two and again in the 1960s and 1970s. Labour's share grew most rapidly in the later 1930s and then more gradually in the 1960s and 1970s.[76] In the world's biggest capitalist economy, the USA, the richest 1% owned 42% and the richest 10% owned 77% of the country's aggregate wealth in 2012, a little higher than in 1917. That proportion has gone up (the 1920s), down (the 1930s and 1940s), up (1950s), down (1960s and 1970s) and up (ever since 1986) over that period, varying between 63% and 84%.[77]

Anyone acquainted with political and working class history will recognise the common factor across Britain, France and the USA in the struggle between capital and labour for national income share: the ability of organised workers to negotiate, take action and secure advances and reforms in the workplace, the economy and society more widely.

This is not the whole explanation, but it is no coincidence that labour made progress in Britain between 1910 and 1920, when periods of growing workplace trade union organisation and militancy before and after the war won major advances in pay, hours and — to a lesser degree — welfare reform, before state-monopoly capitalism launched a major offensive from 1920. Reinvigorated workplace organisation and Labour government reforms tipped the balance away from capital during the long post-World War Two expansion.

In France, inter-war trade union militancy culminated in the extensive reforms of the Popular Front governments of 1936-38. Communist-led post-war trade union militancy and radicalisation of the working class movement produced substantial social and legislative gains in the 1960s and 1970s, although the Union of the Left government of the early 1980s embraced monetarist policies, compelling the French Communist Party to resign from it.

In the USA, after the savage repression of the early 1920s followed by the Wall Street Crash and the Depression, the working class movement fought heroically in the 1930s and 1940s to win a bigger share of the value it created. Cold War anti-communism and anti-socialism combined with treacherous trade union leadership reversed many of those gains until the reaction began to lose its grip in the 1960s.

Thus some supporters of the 'relative' pauperisation thesis point out that elsewhere in *Capital* and other works, Marx was exposing capitalism's drive and tendency towards absolute pauperisation — while he also insisted that this can be checked and reversed if workers are able and willing to revolt, to fight in their trade union and political organisations for a greater share of the value they produce. Indeed, this is the message of his famous lectures published as Wages, Price and Profit (1865), which explains why the wages struggle is necessary in order to increase real wages at the expense of surplus value, while recognising that such gains can never be permanent under capitalism and its wages system.[78]

Most studies bear out the view that trade unionism, fiscal and legislative reforms and the changing nature of work have succeeded in reducing inequalities in income in the advanced capitalist economies over time, but — as Marx warned — these gains are always precarious and subject to reversal.

Some relativists argue that any trend towards absolute pauperisation will also be undermined by changes in the work process and the composition of the labour force. Again, echoing Marx, they point to the growing proportion of the working class engaged in non-manual, technical, clerical, commercial and other service work, much of which will tend to be less arduous and (in some categories only initially according to Marx) better paid than that of the unskilled and semi-skilled labourer or machine operative.

So what of 'the working class, a class always increasing in numbers, and disciplined, united, organised by the very mechanism of the process of capitalist production itself'?

The world's labour force numbers 3.4bn today, compared with no more than 300m in the mid-19th century. Of these, more than 590m are organised in trade unions affiliated to the International Confederation of Trade Unions (176m), the World Federation of Trade Unions (92m) or the All-China Federation of Trade Unions (308m). The highest densities are to be found in the Scandinavian countries, where more than 60% of workers are unionised, followed by Belgium (54%), Cyprus (48%), Ukraine (44% but falling), Italy (35%) and the Russian Federation (down to 31%). In countries such as the Netherlands, Germany, Spain, Portugal and Ireland, union membership may not be very high, but many more workers are covered by trade union bargaining agreements. In many of the most industrialised economies, density has been in decline since the 1950s as the unions have struggled to make ground in the newer service industries and among the many more part-time, temporary and women workers. The proportion of workers in unions is at its lowest ebb in the former socialist countries such as Bulgaria (14%), Poland (12%), the Czech Republic (11%), Slovakia (11%) and Hungary (9%). More encouragingly, Latin America has seen some of the biggest increases in union density over recent decades, led by Bolivia, Chile and Uruguay. The rapidly growing All-China Federation of Trade Unions now embraces 45% of the country's workers, while Cuba's claims 81%, although their approaches and priorities are different to those of unions in capitalist countries, where unions face hostile employers and state institutions.[79]

Of course, as Marx would have been the first to point out, membership numbers are much less important than whether unions fight for the interests of their members, within capitalism and in the political class struggle for socialism. Despite ebbs and flows in militancy, they display no significant loss of capacity and willingness to revolt against significant aspects of capitalism. In many countries, trade union, social and political movements and struggles have challenged capitalist interests to achieve real and substantial advances in working class living standards, democratic rights and the quality of life. Usually on the basis of mass protest against capitalist policies, the working class and its allies have elected social-democratic, socialist and Communist governments that have brought about far-reaching reforms to this effect in many countries since 1917. This was true in the case of welfare and other reforms in developed countries and in the transformation of societies in the Soviet Union and Eastern Europe. In China, Communist Party rule on the basis of economic planning and extensive public ownership has lifted more than 700m people out of extreme poverty in just 20 years: poverty reduction on a scale 'unequalled in history', according to the World Bank.[80]

Supporters of the 'absolutist' perspective can point out that, in purely numerical terms, there is a bigger mass of people exploited and oppressed today than in Marx's time, if only because the world's population is now six times bigger (7.5bn) than it was in 1850 (1.2bn). In a world that produces enough food for everyone, 795m people suffer chronic undernourishment, although the number has fallen rapidly over recent decades.[81] Furthermore, in 2015 there were still 736m people (10% of the global population) living in extreme poverty (with incomes below $1.90 per day), although this is fewer than when *Capital* was first published (about 1.2bn) and again the figure has declined significantly since 1990 (1.85bn or 36%). However, the World Bank has added two new poverty lines to its surveys and now estimates that almost 2bn people (26%) were living on less than \$3.20 a day in 2015.[82]

On the negative side of capitalism's balance sheet must also be entered its responsibility for two world wars and countless colonial and other conflicts, together with imperialist exploitation and debt bondage in the Third World, wide-scale environmental despoliation, global warming and extreme weather conditions and the migrations of many millions of people who have no positive option but to flee the consequences of capitalism's impact on their societies of origin.

Utsa Patnaik (2012) integrates these realities into a powerful case for the absolute pauperisation perspective, at least as far as large parts of the less developed world (the 'South') are concerned. She argues that the process of 'primitive accumulation' of capital now underway in India, China and elsewhere is taking placed in conditions of imperialist globalisation, without the options of utilising slave labour in the colonies and exporting surplus labour (dispossessed peasants, farmers and the rural unemployed) available to the colonial powers during their earlier industrialisation. She throws doubt on the consistency and integrity of official poverty and well-being statistics from the World Bank and national governments, insisting that:

> The present phase of global capitalist accumulation is producing absolute immiserisation and increasing poverty of the masses in the South even as their ruling elites are integrated into the global elite in a subordinate status. The policy-makers of virtually every developing country today have suborned themselves to implement the policies serving finance capital at the expense of the welfare of the mass of their own population. The crucial indicators of welfare are employment and food security. Under neo-liberal policy packages, employment growth has been severely hit in developing countries, while food and nutritional security have been severely undermined. One cannot think of any indicators of welfare which are more important than being employed productively, and obtaining enough income to consume basic necessities like food and clothing in adequate amounts, while availing oneself of minimum medical and educational facilities. Yet these are precisely the indicators which have shown consistent deterioration in the large labour-surplus economies, India and China, over the last two decades; while the exploitation of sub-Saharan Africa has led to an even larger decline in nutritional security over a shorter period of time.[83]

In support of both the 'relative' and 'absolute' pauperisation perspectives, it can be pointed out that in an earlier section of Volume I, where Marx provided 'Illustrations of the General Law of Capitalist Accumulation', he made clear that *Capital* is chiefly concerned with the 'worst paid part of the industrial proletariat, and with the agricultural labourers, who together form the majority of the working class'.

He also declared that a 'full elucidation' of the law of capital accumulation as it affects the conditions of the workers should include matters outside the workplace, such as food and housing.[84]

Overall, the experiences of capitalism in the 19th, 20th and early 21st centuries suggest that it tends to generate inequality, relative poverty and at different conjunctures — for many if not for most — absolute poverty, but that this tendency can be checked and even periodically reversed. This tendency cannot be abolished without abolishing capitalism itself, because it arises in the process of capitalist production itself, not in the sphere of distribution. It is the class ownership of the means of production, distribution and exchange which enables a small minority to accumulate the wealth produced by the surplus labour of the working class. The struggle to redistribute that wealth will always need to be waged for as long as capitalism exists, because it is owned and controlled by the capitalist in the very process of its production.

This brings us to the fundamental contradiction which, Marx proclaimed, would sound the system's death knell. Are capitalism's relations of production — notably monopoly capitalist ownership of the means of production, distribution and exchange — substantially holding back the further development of society's productive forces? Yes, but not to the point of preventing such development taking place altogether, and on a significant scale, however enthusiastically some anti-capitalists proclaim otherwise. Yet it cannot be denied, even by pro-capitalists, that we are approaching the point at which capitalism's increasingly parasitic, anarchic, authoritarian, militaristic, anti-social, anti-environmental character means that is proving incapable of solving humanity's most acute problems.

Political economy in the battle of ideas

In his introduction to the *Economic Manuscripts of 1857-58*, Marx set out his view of what should constitute 'political economy' as a field of study, research and analysis. It should encompass all the relations in society between the different classes of people engaged in economic activity, including how and why those relations change in the transition from one mode of production to another. Because each mode of production and its class relations provide the basis for a social, political, legal and cultural superstructure of relations, ideas and institutions, these also comprise 'political economy'. However much they concentrated their work on some of these elements and not on others, this approach had been broadly accepted by Marx's predecessors, from the French physiocrats to such classical capitalist economists as Smith and Ricardo, as well as by contemporaries such as John Stuart Mill.

In respect of Marx, this approach explains why *Capital*, like his earlier economic work, featured scathing and relentless attacks on every aspect of a system which condemned men, women and children to industrial slavery, debilitating poverty, virulent disease and — in most cases — an early death. Putting false modesty aside, he himself declared that *Capital* would be 'without question the most terrible MISSILE that has yet been hurled at the heads of the bourgeoisie (landowners included)'.[85]

Whether the content or its complexity was responsible, publication of *Das Kapital* in September 1867 met initially with a wall of silence. Frederick Engels wrote reviews to break through it. Friends secured the appearance of translated extracts in English and French journals. Then a Russian translation was produced before a second German edition came out in 1871, after all one thousand copies of the first edition had been sold. Marx edited a French translation and significantly altered the contents. Further editions would appear in English and other languages. The counter-attacks from bourgeois economists eventually arrived, too.

It may also be significant that, after the publication of *Capital*, the case was argued by William Stanley Jevons, Alfred Marshall and other neo-classicists for replacing the term, concept and practice of 'political economy' with that of 'economics'. The latter would deal with the economy as a mathematically informed and logical science, analysing production in terms of laws of supply, demand and utility. In other words, the economy should be studied with the politics of class relations (not least political power) left out.

The ideological struggle over political economy has, of course, continued since Marx's day. However, in recent decades the perceived failure of socialism and Marxism in the Soviet Union and Eastern Europe, together with the triumph of neo-liberalism, has had a profound impact in one arena where the battle has often been fiercest, namely, in the universities, not least in Britain. Economics departments have been turned into 'business schools' and, in many of them, curricula have narrowed to the point where the only theory being studied is neo-liberalism and its classical antecedents. Marxist and Keynesian political economy — previously taught alongside classical and neo-classical theories — has been ruthlessly excluded.

Yet the neo-liberal orthodoxy was tarnished by the 2007-08 financial crash and subsequent economic recession. The high priests of monetarism, free markets, deregulation and privatisation neither foresaw the calamity whose size was precipitated, at least to some degree, by their creed. Nor could they propose any remedy, other than a retreat into an even more fundamentalist laissez-faire cul-de-sac that would have consigned whole economies to ruin. Economics students wondered why their studies were largely restricted to such dogma.

Notably, some of those at the University of Manchester formed a Post-Crash Economics Society in 2010, which is now part of a Rethinking Economics movement with groups in the USA, Germany, France, Brazil, India, Italy, Turkey and China.[86]

After taking part in a debate at the Manchester Union in October 2013, on the motion 'Has Capitalism Failed?', students informed me that little had changed in their courses. Following a debate on the same motion at the University of Bath in March 2015, one of the organisers wrote to tell me: 'A lot of the economists in the audience felt that you transcended their previous knowledge on economics (it is a very narrowly taught subject at university). I think they really valued seeing economics from a fresh perspective'.[87] When I studied Economics and Administration at the same institution in 1970-74, the curriculum featured Marxist political economy and Soviet economic policy as well as the full range of pro-capitalist theories from

Smith and Ricardo to Alfred Marshall, Keynes and Joan Robinson. Now, for the time being, it seems that neo-liberalism exercises its intellectual dictatorship there as elsewhere.

This is all the more reason for communists, socialists, the left and the labour movement to mount a fight-back in the battle of ideas in political economy. But this should not be confined to universities. In the trade unions and political parties of the left, inspired by *Capital*, Marxist political economy at both the theoretical and policy levels now needs to be studied and formulated on a higher level than it is today.

'Productive' and 'unproductive' labour

In numerous passages in *Capital* and the *Economic Manuscript of 1861-63*, Marx drew a distinction between 'productive' and 'unproductive' labour. He did so not in order to elevate one kind above the other as a mark of superiority. Rather, he exposed it as an essential, distinguishing feature of capitalism that most labour power is exchanged for (variable) capital in order to create surplus value — and so is 'productive' from the standpoint of the capitalist — while other labour power is not. As Marx explained:

> Productive labour is only an abbreviation for the whole relation in which, and the manner in which, labour capacity figures in the capitalist production process. It is however of the highest importance to distinguish between this and other kinds of labour, since this distinction brings out precisely the determinate form of labour on which there depends the whole capitalist mode of production, and capital itself. Productive labour, therefore, is labour which — in the system of capitalist production — produces surplus value for its EMPLOYER or which converts the objective conditions of labour into capital, and their owners into capitalists, hence labour which produces its own product as capital.[88]

Such 'productive' labour power has to be engaged in the production of commodities whose value — including the unpaid-for surplus value — can then be realised in money form before, in part at least, being reinvested as capital. While most commodities in Marx's time took a solid, material form (as industrial 'goods'), today many often take the less tangible form of 'services'.

For Marx, therefore, public sector workers who do not produce commodities are 'unproductive' in the capitalist sense, in that they do not create surplus value for a capitalist employer (although it can be argued that they contribute to its creation indirectly by helping to nurture, sustain, educate, train and replenish labour power in general). But whereas the teacher in a state school is therefore 'unproductive', so the teacher in a private school produces surplus value for its capitalist owner in the same respect as does a worker in a sausage factory.[89]

Moreover, in *Capital* Volume I Marx emphasised that the concept of 'productive labour' under capitalism should not be confined to manual labour: 'In order to labour productively, it is no longer necessary for you to do manual work yourself; enough, if you are an organ of the collective labourer, and perform one of its subordinate functions'.[90] In the *1861-63 Manuscript*, he counts the unskilled factory labourer, the overseer and the engineer as organs of the collective labourer, all helping to create surplus value in addition to the value equivalent to their wages.[91] This is where Marx's categorisations become less clear-cut and more contentious. What of labour involved in storing or transporting commodities, guarding or conserving their surplus value and making it realisable in the market? As Gough (1972) shows with great clarity, Marx's view is that this work contributes to a commodity's use-value to the final consumer by rendering the commodity in a more beneficial condition or place.[92] Thus it is productive labour, having a direct impact on the magnitude of a commodity's exchange-value: the transport worker, for instance, adds value partly by transferring value from the means of transportation and partly by adding the value of her or his own labour (some of which will be unpaid, surplus labour to the benefit of the employer).[93]

But where labour can be separated from every sphere of production and is purely concerned in buying and selling, Marx discounts it as a source of use-value within the commodity for sale and therefore of exchange-value, including surplus value. Thus he regarded clerical and accountancy work, for instance, as unproductive labour in the capitalist sense. Today, we might add marketing and retail. Nonetheless, the industrial capitalist deems such labour necessary and is prepared to pay for it. But, as Marx also explains, this industrial capitalist is not buying such labour services as a source of surplus value, for which capital is laid out with the intention of making a profit from it. No, the exchange of money for labour services is the same as occurs when a worker buys labour services. The worker is a consumer, not an exploiter laying out capital for it to expand in the production process, creating surplus value (s) in addition to reproducing its own value (v). The worker and the industrial capitalist both buy labour services for the same purpose, namely, to consume their use-value. In the case of the capitalist consumer, this particular type of use-value cannot pass into the exchange-value of the final commodity being produced for sale, because it has no use-value for the end consumer.

For the commercial capitalist whose clerical workers provide the labour service, this provides the opportunity to capture a share of the surplus value created by the industrial capitalist's workforce. (Similarly, banks and real estate companies capture a share of the industrial capitalist's surplus value in the form of interest and rent). This is the use-value of commercial labour to the commercial capitalist who employs it. As Marx puts it: 'The unpaid labour of these clerks, while it does not create surplus-value, enables him [the commercial capitalist — RG] to appropriate surplus-value ... It is therefore a source of profit to him'.[94] Out of this surplus value, too, comes the revenue from which the commercial labour is paid. Again, according to Marx's analysis:

> Merchant's capital is simply capital functioning in the sphere of circulation. The process of circulation is a phase of the total process of reproduction. But no value is produced in the process of circulation, and, therefore, no surplus value. Only changes of form of the same mass of value take place.[95]

For the industrial capitalist, whether labour services are secured from in-house employees or from outside, these labour costs and the commercial capitalist profit are an expense to be paid from the surplus value created by productive labour.[96]

The commercial worker providing 'unproductive' labour services, whether employed by the industrial or the commercial capitalist, faces the same exploitative pressure as the so-called 'productive' worker. The capitalist employer seeks to minimise the cost in wages of the unproductive labour power and to maximise the use-value extracted from it. In either case, the worker receives a wage that is less than equivalent to the value that would be created in the same working day by a productive worker. In Volume III of *Capital*, Marx gives the example of a commercial worker who produces no surplus value directly, but whose wage is determined by the value of her or his labour power, ie., by the price of its production ...

> while the application of this labour power, its exertion, expenditure of energy, and wear and tear, is as in the case of every other wage labourer by no means limited by its value. His wage, therefore, is not necessarily proportionate to the mass of profit which he helps the capitalist to realise. What he costs the capitalist and what he brings in for him, are two different things. He creates no direct surplus value, but adds to the capitalist's income by helping him to reduce the cost of realising surplus value, inasmuch as he performs partly unpaid labour.[97]

The commercial worker toils for eight hours, say, but receives a wage equivalent to the value created by four hours of society's average necessary labour time. The other four hours comprise 'surplus labour' performed for free for the capitalist, as may be the case with the 'productive' worker.

All workers, whether manual or non-manual, skilled or unskilled, 'productive' or 'unproductive', perform surplus labour under capitalism — and all share a common class interest, namely, to overthrow the capitalist mode of production and put an end to their own exploitation. This necessity becomes more evident as capitalism develops, Marx argued, because advances in office work and in science, education, technology and training tend over time to devalue commercial wages in relation to the average, thereby putting an end to any higher status.

Public sector workers, too, in the non-commodity as well as in any commodity producing branches (where in the latter case they thus create surplus value), provide surplus labour in performing necessary functions for the maintenance and perpetuation of capitalist society. They share the same class interests as other workers.

Crises of disproportion

In examining the circulation of money and capital in detail in Volume II, Marx exposed capitalism's innate susceptibility to imbalance and crisis. Mismatches of supply and demand can occur in each circuit at every stage. Within a particular branch or across the economy as a whole, there can be an excess or a deficiency of money-capital to employ all the forces of production available: costs and prices will go up or down accordingly, affecting profits to a greater or lesser degree. When most commodity production only takes place in order to make a profit, then there will be knock-on effects on further production, investment, employment, wages, demand and so on and on.

Marx attached particular significance to imbalances between the two main departments of the capitalist economy: that producing the means of production for sale to other capitalists (Department I) and that producing the necessities of life (the 'means of subsistence') for workers and — including luxuries — for capitalists, together with their dependants (Department II). Many of the products of Department I require large outlays and longer production times; their deployment often necessitates substantially bigger inputs. Such Department I 'producer' or 'capital' goods cannot be ordered, produced and deployed at short notice. Yet a glut or a shortage of Department I products can have a serious impact on capitalists, workers and the economy as a whole. Yet the decisions about investment, production and employment are not planned in order to balance the two departments over the branch or economy as a whole — let alone to meet society's needs. They are left to individual capitals to arrange and decide in a situation of market anarchy.

The result can be crises of disproportion, where there is a glut or a shortage of Department I products within particular branches of the economy. The result will often be cut-backs in production together with lay-offs and redundancies in one or other or both departments. As demand in the economy shrinks accordingly, so it can spark a downward spiral into recession.

The 'price of production'

In a number of important respects, Volume III — supplemented extensively by Engels — draws together vital elements of Marxist political economy that are of critical significance today.

First, it resolves the seeming paradox by which capitalists in one branch of industry laying out a significantly larger share of their total capital (c + v) on the means of production (c) than in more labour-intensive branches, nonetheless enjoy more or less the same rate of return (ie., profit in proportion to capital used up). Even more incongruously, the average rate of return in Department I — some branches of which have a particularly high organic composition of capital (of c in relation to v) — also tends to approximate to that in Department II. Yet if living labour is the only source of surplus value and therefore profit, the less labour-intensive branches and departments should receive a lower rate of return.

Marx explained that this did not occur, not because the Labour Theory of Value was wrong. Price is still formed in a definite relationship to value (ie., average socially necessary labour time) and profit and surplus value still originate from living labour in the production process. But prices settle around what he called the 'price of production', which represents the cost of production (c + v regardless of their proportions) plus the average rate of profit on the capital laid out on means of production and labour power across the whole economy.

In practice, this means that commodities in branches with a higher organic composition of capital (more c in proportion to v) tend to sell at an average price above their value, while those in more labour-intensive branches sell at an average price below their value. This enables branches with a high proportion of c to capture some of the surplus value that labour-intensive branches contribute to society's total mass of s across the entire economy. A similar price mechanism exists for transferring surplus value within each branch of the economy, so that more mechanised and productive companies — whose units therefore contain less value than the branch average — reap higher returns as a result of selling their own lower-value (and therefore lower cost) units at the price of production for that branch as a whole.

Obviously, in real life there are other factors which also affect market prices: an excess of demand or supply, monopoly power, fashion, etc.

The tendency of the rate of profit to fall

In Part VII of *Capital* Volume I, Marx had considered how capitalist production expands, reproducing itself on an ever more extensive scale as the amount of capital accumulates and is reinvested in means of production and labour power. In Volume III Part III, he analysed this process in detail, setting out one of the most profound laws of Marxist political economy: the tendency for the rate of profit to fall (TRPF).

Marx explained that the means of production (plant, machinery, tools, raw materials, etc.) used up in the economy tend to grow in proportion to the amount of labour power employed. This is the case, whether measured in terms of the value of constant capital expended on the means of production (c) as a proportion of the total capital in the economy as a whole (c plus the variable capital v laid out on living labour power), which Marx called the 'organic composition of capital' (OCC), or in terms of the mass of means of production in proportion to the labour force (the 'technical composition of capital'). The main cause of the tendency of the OCC to rise is the onward march of mechanisation, itself driven by the competition between capitalists to produce more cheaply and capture more market share — and therefore profit — than their rivals. As a worker's labour time can only be increased to a finite extent, Department I acquires an ever-growing significance in the economy because machinery, power, tools etc. can both increase labour productivity and reduce the value (and so real cost to the capitalist) of labour power by reducing the value of its means of subsistence. Yet, at the same time, this department in particular tends to be less labour-intensive and so less productive of surplus value.

Here is why the rising OCC presents an enormous problem for capitalist economies: only the wage-capital invested in labour power can generate fresh surplus value, yet its share in the capital employed across the whole economy is declining. The overall effect of c increasing in proportion to v, therefore, will be the tendency of the rate of profit to fall in the economy overall, as surplus value (s) shrinks as a proportion of capital deployed and consumed (c + v) in the production process.

However, there are countervailing influences that can check the TRPF and 'paralyse its effects'.[98] They increase the absolute or the relative surplus value extracted from labour power. In *Capital* Volume III, Marx elaborates a number of them: intensifying the exploitation of labour (eg., through speeding up the production process and output); depressing wages below the value of labour power; cheapening means of production; and deploying the 'relative' surplus population resulting from higher labour productivity in new lines of mainly labour-intensive production, notably of luxury products. Capitalists may also seek to grow the mass of profit to compensate for the falling rate of profit — although this will generate yet more surplus capital and tends, in less labour-intensive branches of production, to increase the OCC over time, thereby depressing the rate of profit still further. Raising labour productivity through the introduction of more machinery or enhanced technology usually has the same effect, notably where the rising OCC outstrips the rising rate of exploitation. It should also be borne in mind that while there may be considerable scope for extending mechanisation and the application of new technology, there are physical limits to the rapidity and extent to which labour can be intensified and its productivity increased.

Other countervailing effects to the TRPF can be found in foreign investment and trade. In Volume I of *Capital*, Marx had noted that capital which cannot make any or sufficient profit at home might be sent abroad 'because it can be employed at a higher rate of profit in a foreign country'.[99] As he elaborated in a section on foreign trade in Volume III, capital invested in cheap labour abroad ('slaves, coolies, etc.') to produce cheap imports into the home country may yield a higher rate of profit than the norm domestically, thereby equalising the general rate of profit. Imports generally can cheapen the means of production domestically and — by reducing the price of necessities — also cheapen the cost of labour power at home, thereby raising the domestic rate of profit. Capital invested in the home production of highly competitive exports from a more advanced economy may earn a 'super profit'. However, insofar as these operations accelerate the accumulation of capital for investment in the home market, they will tend over the long run to increase the OCC and intensify the TRPF.[100]

In reality, too, mechanisation increases the proportion of c in relation to v in the production process as a whole, despite the employment of extra labour in Department I to produce the additional or enhanced means of production.

Does this mean that automation through 'artificial intelligence' and robotics might eventually displace a very large proportion of the workforce, proceeding — if only exponentially — towards an economy of nil employment and therefore nil production of surplus value? A recent Organisation for Economic Co-operation and Development (OECD) study challenges previous claims that up to 47% of jobs in the USA could disappear because of automation. It puts the — still significant — proportion of 'highly automatable' jobs (ie., at 70% or higher risk of automation) at 14% in the USA, Britain, Japan and other advanced economies. The OECD analysts identified unskilled and young workers as the most likely victims, arguing that many mechanised jobs also involve ancillary managerial, supervisory and interpersonal tasks that cannot be performed satisfactorily by robots or computers.[101]

Marx himself did not believe that the accumulation of capital would reach the point of replacing most if not all living labour. Instead, he reasoned, the price of labour power will fall and make it profitable to employ it once again, either in existing branches of the economy or in new ones if necessary.[102] It could be added that capitalism would be unlikely to survive as a mode of production should a large section of society revolt against a system that could only guarantee long-term mass unemployment without the means with which to lead a tolerable and productive life.

While countervailing tendencies can slow, suspend and even reverse the falling rate of profit, they cannot abolish its tendency to fall. This tendency asserts and reasserts itself, even though the rate of exploitation (the rate of surplus value: s/v) may be rising, as the value of labour falls and mechanisation raises productivity, requiring less living labour for each unit of output. Indeed, Marx maintained that there was a tendency for the rate of surplus value to rise although this, too, had countervailing tendencies — not least the fight of workers for higher wages, for shorter hours with no loss of pay, etc. — and did not outweigh the TRPF. Because the tendencies of more intensive exploitation and falling profit rates not only co-exist but reinforce one another, he insisted that 'nothing is more absurd, for this reason, than to explain the fall in the rate of profit by a rise in the rate of wages'.[103]

In *Capital* Volume III, Marx pointed out that the 'immediate purpose and compelling motive' of capitalist production is to produce surplus value, not to produce things because the capitalist class or other people will enjoy them, or because the population needs those products in order to survive.[104] And yet, commodities will only yield their surplus value when purchased by their intended consumers in Department I and Department II. However, full consumption and the full realisation of surplus value are not guaranteed, especially for the commodities produced in Department II which depend upon the purchasing power of workers in both departments. That power is restricted by the drive to maximise the rate of exploitation, further limiting its ability to keep up with the expansion of labour productivity and commodity production. Here lies the link between the TRPF and cyclical crisis. Periodically, the point is reached where commodities cannot be sold at a profit; nor can labour power (itself a commodity) be employed at a profit. The result is a crisis of the over-accumulation of capital and the over-production of commodities.

When the costs of labour power and means of production have fallen sufficiently to raise the rate of exploitation, when the depreciation in capital values enables the formation of new capital that can expect a higher rate of profit, production revives and the cycle proceeds towards growth, boom and the next recession and possibly slump.

A number of studies confirm the operation of the TRPF in Britain and other capitalist economies, in fact across the international capitalist economy in total.

Perhaps the best summary of calculations of Britain's rate of profit as Marx understood it can be found in a paper by Michael Roberts (2015a): [105]

UK rate of profit 1855-2009 (%)

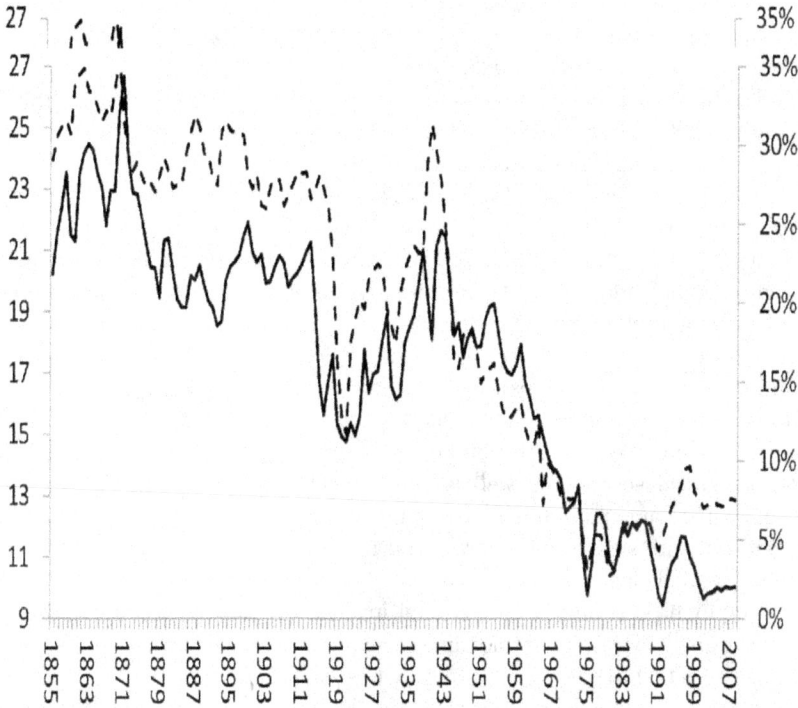

ONS-BOE = Office for National Statistics/Bank of England (left-side scale)
Maito-RHS = Esteban Maito (2014)[106] (right-side scale)

Roberts (2015a) estimates that it has fallen from an average of 24% of capital consumption in the late 1850s and 1860s to 10% by the 2007 crash. This downward trend has been cyclical, spanning approximately 17 short cycles and four long ones. The biggest and sharpest drops occurred in the 1870s, 1912-16 (just before and during the first half of the Great Imperialist War), 1930-32 (after the Wall Street Crash) and 1944-49 (from the end of the Second World War and into the reconstruction). Between the end of that war and 1975, the rate of profit in Britain fell in cycles from almost 22% to less than 10%. This was, of course, a period in which strong shop floor trade unionism and a hugely expanded welfare state raised both the workplace and 'social' wage in real terms, at the expense of corporate profits, as workers successfully resisted attempts to raise the rate of exploitation.

Between the late 1970s and 1996, monetarist and neo-liberal policies increased the rate of exploitation (s/v) by 56%, producing a higher rate of profit (up by 20%), despite a sizeable increase (46%) in the organic composition of capital. But the impact of that higher OCC, supplemented by a further but smaller economic growth to 2008, together with an increase in real workplace and social wages (largely as the result of the first-term Labour government policies), both halted the rise in the exploitation rate and reduced the rate of profit by 14%. Roberts (2015a) shows that across the post-war period, from 1946 to 2008, the rate of surplus value rose by 8%, yet the rate of profit fell by 46% as the OCC increased by 182%. His figures demonstrate that the rate of profit declines when the OCC rises faster than the rate of exploitation, fully in keeping with Marx's Theory of Surplus Value.

Maito (2014) has calculated the average rate of profit in six core countries (Britain, the USA, Germany, Netherlands, Japan and Sweden) between 1869 and 2009. The difficulty of finding complete and reliable data means he measures net profits as a proportion of the outlay on fixed constant capital alone (that part of c spent replacing and expanding machinery, plant and buildings), but not on circulating constant capital (the part of c spent on tools and inputs such as materials and power) plus variable capital v (the outlay on wages). Although this raises the rate of profit figures, the enormous preponderance of fixed capital over variable capital and the accelerating speed with which the circulating and variable capital turn over in production, means that his approach serves quite well as a measure of the movement in the rate of profit over time. The same pattern is replicated in Britain, albeit at a generally lower rate of profit, but with steeper falls during and immediately after the two world wars, a sharper rise in the late 1930s and an unusually heavy decline in the 1950s and 1960s (reflecting high post-war levels of capital investment, the 'welfare state' consensus and the strength of shop floor trade unionism and collective bargaining).

Maito finds that the average rate of profit — as he calculates it — in the six core countries has experienced a downward trend historically, from around 42% in 1869 to 12% in 2010. There was a sharp drop during the 1929-33 Great Depression, a prolonged and substantial decline from 1969 to 1983 (when the working class movements in the US and Western Europe were at the peak of their strength economically and politically), and a slight recovery and semi-stabilisation to 2007. He also finds that the TRPF runs through both short (usually around five or six years) and long (40-50 years) cycles, confirming the research by Minqi Li and others (2007).[107] Calculations for the rate of return in eight 'peripheral' economies of mostly smaller, developing or Third World countries from the mid-1950s show the same downward trend — but at levels roughly twice those of the core countries. Roberts (2015b) has calculated average rates of profit for the world and for the G7 biggest capitalist economies between 1963 and 2008 using Marx's formula. Both show an identical decline to 1975, followed by a continuous — except for the late 1970s and early 1980s — but partial recovery to a peak in 1988, followed by a fall and then recovery in the mid-1990s before the 2007 drop.[108]

However, Maito's estimates claim no long-term TRPF in the USA in the course of the 20th and early 21st centuries. While the short and longer cycles are evident and as pronounced as elsewhere, profit levels have been a little higher in the second half of the period than in the first. But it should also be noted that US profit levels had dropped hugely during the 1880s and were always significantly lower than in Britain (until 1945) and Germany (until the early 1960s). Other studies have calculated US surplus value and its proportionality to total capital consumption more precisely, using the most up to date figures available for the post-World War Two period. For instance, Peter Jones (2013) confirms that the rate of profit has yet to fully recover from its heavy falls in the 1950s, late 1960s and 1970s.[109] Michael Roberts (2011) shows that only when the organic composition of capital declined, from the very late 1950s until 1966 and then from the early 1980s to the end of the century, did the rate of profit — which he calculates in accordance with the Marxist definition — climb back upwards. Roberts (2011) reveals the same inverse relationship between the rate of profit and the OCC in his estimates for Britain between 1855 and 1914.[110]

Comprehensive calculations by Themistoklis Kalogerakos (2013) show — cycles aside — a downward trend in the US corporate rate of profit between 1965 and 1980, followed by a smaller upturn and then levelling off. His figures prove conclusively over a 60-year period that corporate profit rates in the non-financial sector rise when the OCC falls, and vice-versa, in patterns of almost perfect inverse symmetry whether for cycles or trend.[111]

Most calculations for the British economy and internationally demonstrate that Marx's theory of the TRPF holds true, and that his whole Theory of Surplus Value — and within it the significance of the OCC — explains the origin and trajectory of capitalist profit.

Piketty versus *Capital*

This is very different from the non-Marxist, anti-communist and anti-Soviet liberalism served up by Thomas Piketty in his *Capital in the Twenty-first Century* (2014). While this substantial volume is a triumph of research and data reconstruction, its flaws are near fatal. He redefines 'capital' to make no distinction between wage-capital (which directly exploits labour power), rentier capital and fictitious capital on the one side, and 'state capital' in a socialist economy on the other. It is only the latter two (fictitious and socialist 'state' capital) that he finds objectionable; the first of them because it is non-productive and captures too much of the wealth (at the expense of labour and 'productive' capital and land — a piece of classical bourgeois economic theory), the second because it offends his liberal sensibilities. His focus is on the grossly unequal distribution of wealth — growing since 1950 and concealed and underestimated — which he regards as a mortal threat to democracy and productive capitalist entrepreneurship. Piketty divorces the distribution of value and wealth from its mode of production and attaches no significance to Marx's theories of value and the TRPF. Nor does he ascribe any role to the working class, its unions or its political parties in past, present and future struggles to redistribute wealth.[112]

Despite its title, Piketty's work has nothing in common with Marx's *Capital* and has more in common, ideologically with the radical Liberalism of David Lloyd George. Not surprisingly, therefore, it won the *Financial Times* and McKinsey 'Business Book of the Year' award in 2014. In the book, he proposes a global tax on capital, which he admits is 'utopian' and 'unrealistic' but has the merit of being 'far less dangerous' than the alternatives such as national 'capital controls', which would threaten 'economic openness' (ie., capitalist globalisation). Piketty's fall-back position is, therefore, to move towards a global capital tax by beginning at, say, the European level. This despite the reality that the European Union is one of the least likely bodies on earth to move against the interests of monopoly capital in such a way. He makes no mention of the wealth taxes that still operate — however imperfectly — in countries such as his own (France), Norway, Argentina and the Swiss cantons (neo-liberalism secured their abolition in seven other Western European countries) and which have long been under consideration in Britain.[113] Like Lloyd George, Piketty sounds like a radical but that is because he wants to propose a credible alternative to socialism, not to capitalism.

Nonetheless, his research provides ammunition for readers who might prefer to draw revolutionary conclusions from it. His call for an albeit impractical global tax on capital propelled the principle of wealth redistribution into headlines across the developed capitalist world. This might explain the subsequent counter-attacks led by former Bank of England Governor Mervyn King and the *Financial Times* itself, although Piketty's riposte forced the latter into a humiliating retreat.[114]

Theoretical controversies

Marx had already made clear his view, in the Introduction to the *Economic Manuscripts of 1857-58*, that political economy could only be understood and analysed by employing concepts such as 'labour' and 'value' in models that are abstracted from reality. This enables different things to be identified and studied dialectically, in their dynamic relations with each other and within the totality. Having clarified definitions, assessments, etc. models and their conceptions can then be applied to reality in an effort to understand that reality fully and dynamically.

In Volume III of *Capital* as elsewhere, Marx used mathematical quantities and equations to illustrate the mechanics and tendencies of capitalism's political economy. This has opened the door to schools of thought within and outside the Marxist tradition which claim to have detected mathematical inconsistencies in his theories of falling profit and the translation of input values (of c and v) into their purchase prices of production (the so-called 'Transformation Problem'), especially in the context of capital accumulation and extended reproduction. Some of these critiques appear to rely on contradictions within static models that bear even less relation to economic reality than they do to Marx's own models in Volume III. Perhaps Ben Fine is right to insist that the problem is algebraic and perfectly capable of resolution.[115] Some defenders of Marx's original method are associated with the Temporal Single-System Interpretation (TSSI) of his theories of surplus value and the TRPF.[116]

There are related conceptual controversies, for example, over questions of the quality of labour. In Volume I of *Capital*, Marx contrasted average, 'simple' labour to skilled, 'complex' labour. He treated the latter as merely an intensified, multiplied quantity of the former. This has given rise to intense debate and dispute within Marxist political economy ever since, again, especially when trying to convert labour values into quantities, costs and prices expressed in mathematical proportions and equations. Furthermore, there are controversies around the question of the labour power involved in housework, education and training. To what extent, if any, can it be said that domestic workers, teachers and trainers help in their different ways to produce surplus value by enhancing labour power, and so perform unpaid labour ultimately for the benefit of the capitalist class (bearing in mind that in the first case the value of the average worker's wage includes the means of subsistence for his or her dependants)? [117]

'Under-consumption' and Keynesianism

Because crises of over-production and over-accumulation appear as crises of purchasing power and investment, schools of political economy have arisen which differ from Marx in both diagnosis and remedy. Theories of 'under-consumptionism' within and outside the Marxist tradition emphasise the sphere of circulation as the main source of capitalist crisis, rather than the sphere of production. This leads to the promotion of anti-crisis or counter-cyclical 'remedies' which increase purchasing power through higher wages and more state spending on social benefits, public services and job creation programmes.

Marx himself recognised that under-consumption can legitimately be seen as another side of the same coin. In Volume III of *Capital*, he went so far as to assert that: 'The ultimate reason for all real crises always remains the poverty and restricted consumption of the masses as opposed to the drive of capitalist production to develop the productive forces as though only the absolute consuming power of society constituted their limit'.[118] Even so, he attached primary significance to over-production and over-accumulation as the main source of cyclical crises, as a systemic contradiction that could not be eradicated by maintaining consumption artificially, ie., by trying to permanently inflate purchasing power above the incomes of workers, people generally, the state and the capitalist class.

In response to the 1929-32 Depression, the under-consumptionist theories of John Maynard Keynes in particular won wide support across the political spectrum in the USA (President Roosevelt's 'New Deal'), Britain (post-1945 Labour and Conservative governments) and Western Europe (the Marshall Plan). His General Theory of Employment, Interest and Money (1936) argued that capitalist markets, left to their own devices, do not naturally tend to equilibrium and full employment. Government intervention is necessary — especially during a recession — to stimulate employment and demand, notably through public works programmes funded from government borrowing, taxation or printing money. 'Left' Keynesians placed particular emphasis on nationalisation, the direction of private capital, price controls and taxes on high incomes, wealth and corporate profits to boost demand, investment and employment.

As well as producing contradictory effects such as inflationary price rises, capital flight, tax avoidance, higher interest rates, increased National Debt servicing costs and private sector investment 'strikes' — which compel governments to challenge the power of capital or surrender to it — the under-consumptionist approach postpones the recession and, if not reversed, makes it all the steeper upon arrival.

In terms of controversies of macro-economic theory, mention should be made here of the 'permanent arms economy' theory pioneered within the Marxist tradition by Tony Cliff, Duncan Hallas and, consummately, Michael Kidron.[119] This claimed that relatively high and stable state expenditure on armaments maintained demand in the economies of the main capitalist powers to a significant degree, helping to sustain the long post-1945 expansion. Moreover, it was argued, it did so by absorbing capital into the production process where it could bolster the rate of profit rather than stand idle or depress it. The nature of the product also ensured a high degree of 'built-in' obsolescence, requiring the constant reinvestment of capital on the basis of expanded reproduction.

There were several grave misconceptions and omissions of reality in this variant of 'military Keynesianism', an under-consumptionist theory promoted by Joan Robinson and other left-Keynesians.[120] Not least, it did not convincingly explain why there should be any qualitative difference between state military expenditure and, say, more or less permanent and substantial state spending on infrastructure and prestige 'white elephant' projects. The theory did not take sufficient account of the fact that sustained capitalist growth also took place in countries with low levels of military spending such as West Germany, Sweden and Japan. Nor could it show why capital-intensive military spending should not have accelerated the growth in the OCC, thereby ultimately depressing the rate of profit in the major arms producing economies of the USA, Britain and France and precipitating an earlier and deeper profits crisis in those countries than anywhere else. Furthermore, while arms exports add substantially to the profits of that particular branch of the domestic economy, they also add to the surplus capital that subsequently needs to be profitably employed. To his credit, Kidron later acknowledged these and other weaknesses in the 'permanent arms economy' theory[121]

Monetarism and neo-liberalism

The reaction to Keynesianism, especially to the potential challenge offered by its 'left' variants, has been the revival and adaptation of classical political economic theory and policy. Since the early 1970s, the ideas of 'monetarism' and 'neo-liberalism' have risen to prominence, associated with the Economics Department of the University of Chicago, Milton Friedman and Frederick Hayek ('the Chicago School') and in Britain the Institute of Economic Affairs and the Adam Smith Institute. They defend the 'efficiency' of 'free markets' and argue that full employment is inflationary because it favours the collective power of trades unions, thereby further distorting the labour market. Their preferred policies include strict control of the money supply; lower government spending and borrowing (to the point of zero-deficit budgets); deregulation and privatisation in place of state controls and public ownership; a more regressive taxation system; and an end to 'distortions' in the labour market caused by trade unions, excessive employment rights and other legislative 'red tape'. The 'market' and 'investors' should once more become sovereign, free from macro-economic planning and other impositions by the bureaucratic, interventionist and incompetent state.

Under the banner of fiscal responsibility and fighting inflation, the chief goal of neo-liberalism has been to reverse the TRPF by increasing the rate of exploitation and thereby raise both the rate and the mass of profit.

For all its ideological propaganda against 'statism', the 'nanny state', etc., neo-liberalism believes strongly in the use of capitalist state power to pursue its preferred policies, whether to repress trade unions, assist the armaments industry, secure free trade and investment agreements, bail out the banks (which some purist neo-liberals reject) or remove a troublesome Third World regime. This intensely ideological and political approach has been seen most starkly in practice where governments have come to office determined to implement neo-liberal policies: Chile in 1973, Britain in 1979 and the USA in 1981. In all three cases, a fierce battle of ideas was conducted against those of Keynesianism, Marxism and all forms of social collectivism. In Chile, advised by Chicago School economists, the military dictatorship of General Pinochet privatised industry and land, reduced taxes for the rich and big business, slashed social spending, abolished controls on the export of capital, brutally suppressed trade unions and the political left ... but succeeded in hugely reducing inflation and restoring profits until economic and financial crisis compelled a part-reversal of policies. In Britain, the adoption of monetarism (which some called 'Thatcherism') took a milder form in terms of tax and spending cuts, privatisation, anti-trade union laws and attempts to control the money supply. In the 1990s, politically and ideologically, the mantle of neo-liberalism passed to the New Labour trend in the Labour Party which rejected social democracy as well as socialism.

In purely economic terms, neo-liberalism succeeded in its immediate mission. The rate of profit — however calculated by different Marxist economists — turned upwards in the early 1980s. It continued on this upward trend, albeit with cyclical slowdowns, until the recession of the early 1990s before recovering once more. In Britain, neo-liberal policies revived the rate of profit in Britain through much of the period between 1982 and 1997. New technology was introduced and trade unionism weakened in order to intensify the rate of exploitation, which at least for a time outstripped the increase in the OCC.[122]

'Fictitious' capital, financialisation and the 'Great Crash'

In Volume III of *Capital*, Marx traced the history and development of capital as a commodity in itself, as money lent at interest ('usury') or used as 'merchant capital' purely to buy and sell goods at a profit without expanding real value in the process. In pre-capitalist modes of production, such money-capital is largely parasitic, battening upon and ultimately helping to dissolve them.

Under capitalism, however, commercial capital performs a range of functions of varying usefulness by financing activities in the spheres of production, circulation and exchange. For example, although the operations of storing, transporting and retailing commodities do not add to their value, such deployment of commercial capital conserves the value already embedded in them and helps to realise it. In doing so, the price the commercial capitalists charge for their services or pay wholesale for goods to be retailed in effect capture a portion of the surplus value already created in the process of production. In that sense, the commercial service is itself a commodity being sold and bought above its own value, while wholesale goods are being exchanged below their value.

As loan capital invested in the production process, commercial capital captures a portion of surplus value in the form of interest on the loan. Share capital represents a legal entitlement to a future portion of surplus value without investing any new capital into the enterprise concerned.

In Chapter XXV (25), Marx quoted examples to show how promissory or credit notes, or 'bills of exchange', between industrial capitalists and merchants themselves form a market in which they are sold and bought. Alongside this, the banks increasingly centralise in their own hands the reserve funds — the loanable money-capital — of businesses, lend it at interest and handle domestic and international payments on behalf of their clients: 'They become the general managers of money-capital' and make their profits by lending at a higher rate of interest than they borrow, taking on bills at a discount and buying interest-bearing government bills, bonds and corporate stocks.[123] Deposits can be extended as loans to borrowers several times over because they are not likely to be drawn upon all at once at short notice by the depositors.

As these operations multiply prolifically, the opportunities for swindling and fraud multiply likewise. Money can be obtained as credit for export goods that might never be sold (or even produced). Shares can be sold that might never yield the promised dividends. Engels added an account of how railway speculation, export fraud and crop failure had created a financial crisis in England in 1847. Bills of exchange went unsold (except at huge discounts), interest rates rocketed and companies went bankrupt.

Marx divides bank capital into, firstly, cash (money, gold or notes) and, secondly, securities (bills of exchange or government bonds, treasury bills, other stocks and shares and mortgages). Yet interest-bearing bank capital is, according to Marx, 'fictitious'. Interest is being received on capital that is purely nominal: it is either a deposit that has already been received and lent out in multiple amounts, or a security that cannot be exchanged for its nominal value, but only at its market price. This is 'fictitious capital', the interest from which represents a claim on the wealth produced by society's surplus labour, while not itself employing labour power to create any surplus value whatsoever in the production process. Moreover, these securities themselves become commodities, to be traded at prices which bear little or no relation to the capital originally laid out on them (and possibly used for investment in production); they depend, instead, on the size and reliability of the interest or dividend payable on them. Speculation then seeks a quick profit from their purchase and sale. Marx noted that:

With the development of interest-bearing capital and the credit system, all capital seems to double itself, and sometimes treble itself, by the various modes in which the same capital, or perhaps even the same claim on a debt, appears in different forms in different hands. The greater portion of this 'money-capital' is purely fictitious. All the deposits, with the exception of the reserve fund, are merely claims on the banker, which, however, never exist as deposits.[124]

Editing this text sometime around 1893, Engels added in a footnote that 'this doubling and trebling of capital has developed considerably further in recent years, for instance, through Financial Trusts, which already occupy a heading of their own in the report of the London Stock Exchange'.[125] While loan capital grows quite independently of the accumulation of real capital, Marx noted in Volume III of *Capital* that the expansion of capital in the production process, in its quest for surplus value, 'breeds overproduction, speculation, crises, and surplus capital alongside surplus population'.[126] In particular, unable to find sufficiently profitable re-investment in production, a portion of this surplus capital seeks other opportunities through its deployment as fictitious banking capital. There is a tendency for speculation in fictitious capital to grow:

> With the development of the credit system, great concentrated money markets are created, such as London, which are at the same time the main seats of trade in this paper. The bankers place huge quantities of the public's money-capital at the disposal of this unsavoury crowd of dealers, and thus this brood of gamblers multiplies.[127]

But this over-accumulation and over-production of real and fictitious capital cannot continue indefinitely, outstripping as it does the over-production of commodities. Equilibrium must be restored through the withdrawal or destruction of capital in the economy. But as his notes on 'Theories of Surplus Value' confirm, Marx also believed that industrial capital would tame interest-bearing capital and — with the assistance of government regulation and planning — subordinate it to the needs of the productive economy.[128] As we know today, that subordination certainly did not happen in the late 20th and early 21st centuries.

The collapse of the socialist economies of the Soviet Union and Eastern Europe opened up new opportunities for the neo-liberal counter-offensive to spread and intensify. Many of the barriers to the movement of Western monopoly capital around the world were dismantled in a process dubbed 'globalisation'. This capitalist or imperialist globalisation was presented as inevitable whereas, in reality, it required the deployment of US, British, German and French state power in order to advance. In particular, the leading imperialist powers combined together in existing international agencies (the European Union, the International Monetary Fund, the World Bank, etc.) and new ones (the World Trade Organisation, the G7 and G20 groups of heads of government and central bank governors) to promote it.

Free from any meaningful controls, especially after Britain's 'Big Bang' deregulation of the City of London in 1986 and repeal of the Glass-Steagall banking legislation in the US in the late 1990s, finance capital engaged in an orgy of fictitious accumulation (in addition to the real accumulation reflected in an upsurge of company mergers and acquisitions). In a process known as 'financialisation', all kinds of financial contracts were turned into interest-bearing but also very complex 'products' such as collateralised debt obligations, to be traded in the liberalised financial markets, notably in the City and on Wall Street.

Speculation further boosted their exchange price so that, by 2007, the market-price 'value' of all financial securities on the world's capital markets would have entitled the holders to consume the real value all the goods and services produced by all the world's economies several times over. Global financial assets totalled $196 trillion, compared with the world's aggregate nominal GDP of $56 trillion.[129] That proportion of 350% had grown from 109% in 1980. In the world's biggest capitalist economy, the total value of all financial assets had risen from five times US GDP in 1980 to ten times by the eve of the Great Crash. In Britain and the Eurozone, the stock of financial assets had reached around 53 and 37 times GDP, respectively, by 2007 and still rising.[130]

Beginning to realise that much of the actual or potential monetary value of these financial 'products' was largely fictitious — much of it relying on the repayment of debt that the debtors would not be able to honour — the holders of securities of various sorts began to dump them in what became the great crash. Thus in August 2007, BNP Paribas opened the first phase of the financial crisis by announcing its withdrawal from three hedge funds engaged in US mortgage debt. A crazy game of 'pass the parcel' began, as nobody wanted to be left holding toxic financial packages, yet could not offload them onto anyone else. The banks ceased lending to themselves and other speculators. Financial institutions began to go under, unable to meet their financial liabilities. In Britain, the Northern Rock mortgage crisis had broken out in September 2007 and the New Labour government nationalised the company in February 2008. The collapse of US investment bank Lehman Brothers in September 2008 opened a new phase in the international financial crisis as Western governments and central banks organised takeovers of failing financial institutions or bailed them out with guarantees for their depositors or public funds to buy their toxic securities at a discount and recapitalise their reserves. Some share purchases amounted to full or partial nationalisation.

Where governments and their central banks could not bail out their own financial institutions, or raise enough money on the financial markets to fund public expenditure commitments (include the interest on state debt), they turned to the EU Commission, the European Central Bank and the IMF (the 'Troika'). The conditions attached to loans by the Troika have been swingeing: social and welfare spending cuts, sweeping privatisations, higher state pension retirement ages and labour 'flexibility' reforms. Similar 'austerity' measures have been carried in other countries in order to fund their domestic bailout programmes. In short, the capitalist states and their international agencies nationalised the private liabilities and privatised the public funds.

This was not how Marx thought things would turn out. As he anticipated in Volume III of *Capital*:

> In a system of production, where the entire continuity of the reproduction process rests upon credit, a crisis must obviously occur — a tremendous rush for means of payment — when credit suddenly ceases and only cash payments have validity. At first glance, therefore, the whole crisis seems to be merely a credit and money crisis. And in fact it is only a question of the convertibility of bills of exchange into money. But the majority of these bills represent actual sales and purchases, whose extension far beyond the needs of society is, after all, the basis of the whole crisis. At the same time, an enormous quantity of these bills of exchange represents plain swindle, which now reaches the light of day and collapses; furthermore, unsuccessful speculation with the capital of other people; finally, commodity capital which has depreciated or is completely unsaleable, or returns that can never more be realised again. The entire artificial system of forced expansion of the reproduction process cannot, of course, be remedied by having some bank, like the Bank of England, give to all the swindlers the deficient capital by means of its paper and having it buy up all the depreciated commodities at their old nominal values. Incidentally, everything here appears distorted, since in this paper world, the real price and its real basis appear nowhere, but only bullion, metal coin, notes, bills of exchange, securities. Particularly in centres where the entire money business of the country is concentrated, like London, does this distortion become apparent; the entire process becomes incomprehensible; it is less so in centres of production.[131]

Economically, the result has been the longest and deepest capitalist recession for 80 years. But was this a purely a financial crash? Or was it connected to the cyclical character of the capitalist economy, a periodic over-accumulation and over-production? Perhaps its origins lay deeper, in the longer term tendency of the OCC to rise and the tendency of the rate of profit to fall reaching a critical point, requiring the large-scale destruction of capital values, both fictitious and real?

The revival of the capitalist rate of profit in the US and Britain in the 1980s and 1990s had released much more capital for speculative purposes, emboldened by a confidence that returns would continue at their higher levels. Yet the organic composition of capital had also revived and the rate of profit in the USA, Britain and other G7 and G20 economies, had begun to fall and then falter from the late 1990s (as productivity gains were counteracted by stiffening competition from Third World and Chinese producers). A further downward turn began in 2005.[132]

Freeman (2012) argues that rate of profit calculations for capitalist economies should include all the capital deployed and profits made in the financial sector, including those derived from the expansion of Marx's 'fictitious capital' (and which play no part in the creation of real surplus value as he understood it, through the exploitation of living labour).[133] Once included, arguably on the same basis as Marx included merchant profit and rent in the general rate of profit and the TRPF, these show an uninterrupted decline in the rate of profit in the USA and Britain — homes of the world's two biggest financial markets — since the late 1960s, with no neo-liberal driven upturn from the early 1980s. According to Freeman and adherents of the TSSI school, this has happened — despite the huge profits made from financialisation — because the huge volume of capital employed across the whole economy (now including its financial markets) lowers the proportion of surplus value (s) in relation to the total capital employed (c + v).

This analysis appears to locate the 2007-08 crash in a classic crisis of over-accumulation and over-production, albeit one of a particularly acute character.

Obversely, it could be argued that this analysis downplays the impact of neo-liberalism and financialisation from the 1980s onwards and the impact of a financial crisis on the unfolding cyclical downturn in the productive economy. In the period leading up to the crash, working class purchasing power had been growing more slowly and, in the case of the US, had remained stagnant. Indeed, it relied increasingly upon soaring household debt that became more difficult to sustain and riskier to finance. Kalogerakos (2013) found that the profit rate of non-financial corporations in the US began a cyclical fall in 2005. In the G7 economies, output peaked in late 2006 and early 2007. After a long period of expansion, the US economy slowed down at the end of 2007, and then shrank in real terms in the first quarter of 2008. In Britain, economic growth came to a halt in the first quarter of 2008 as it did in other areas of the international capitalist economy.[134]

According to Kalogerakos, the share of financial corporations in total US corporate profits had grown steadily from 8% in 1947 before slipping from peaks of 21% in the 1970s to 12% by 1984. From there, however, it more than doubled through the cycles before escalating from the start of the new century to 40% by the year 2000. Significantly, it began its steep collapse in 2001, several years before arriving at a 10% trough in 2007. He estimates that the rate of capital accumulation (which he measures by new constant capital as a proportion of existing fixed capital) lagged well below the recovering rate of profit from 1984, and fell far more sharply than it from 2005, to zero as companies devoted a growing share of their profits to shareholder dividends rather than to new, productivity-driven investment. They also ploughed more of their undistributed profits into the financial sector as opportunities for profitable investment in the productive economy shrank.

All this suggests that financialisation, which was promoted by the wider neo-liberal agenda in favour of corporate profits, further destabilised the downturn of the productive economy. The financial crisis of 2007-08, together with the priority bailout of the financial sector and the accompanying austerity measures, then plunged the international economy from recession into depression, beginning with the most financialised economies of the USA and Britain. In order to begin a recovery, it was necessary for capitalism to destroy 'fictitious capital' values on a large scale, unavoidably devaluing real capital along with them. This has been managed by the capitalist states on an enormous scale and through international coordination in the G7, IMF and EU. Profitability has been restored at minimal expense to the monopoly corporations, but at huge cost to the working class and people generally.

In order to maintain this drive, the capitalist classes and their governments and states are seeking to impose ever more oppressive terms of employment. Many more workers are on part-time, short-term or zero-hour contracts while migrant and mobile labour is super-exploited in order to undermine wages, pensions, standards, trade unionism and collective bargaining. In its 2019 World Development Report, for instance, the World Bank proposes wide-ranging measures to 'reform' the labour market, increase flexibility and intensify exploitation across the world.[135] These include cutting and breaching statutory minimum pay levels, reducing corporate contributions to the 'social wage', allowing employers to enrol new employees on sub-normal wages and minimising protection for workers against dismissal.[136] The financial responsibility for ensuring adequate education, training and income at each stage in life should fall almost entirely on the population generally, through expenditure taxes such as VAT rather than on higher-level incomes. Children's schooling is considered primarily from the standpoint of their future productivity in employment, complete with detailed financial calculations.

In true neo-liberal fashion, the World Bank report characterises every aspect of society as 'capital'. Thus people are regarded mainly as 'human capital', to be invested in and made more productive as present or future workers, while social provision is 'social capital' for the same purposes. It is a totalitarian world-view, intended to disguise and normalise capitalist exploitation as the central, defining and permanent feature of human society.

The contradiction at the core of the World Bank perspective for capitalist economic growth is that of capitalism itself. Expanding both the mass and the rate of profit — at least until the TRPF reasserts itself — will precipitate an over-accumulation of capital which will, in turn, further stimulate financialisation and its prolific generation of fictitious capital. In the absence of far stricter regulation of the financial markets and institutions, the scene is being set for another financial crisis. The warning signs have already appeared. In the run-up to the international recession of 2000-01, the global amount of capital value engaged in corporate mergers and acquisitions (M&As) soared from $397bn in 1991 to $4,115bn eight years later. Then an international recession broke, the dot.com bubble burst and the capital engaged in M&As was cut in half. The value of M&As then rose to a new all-time high of $4,290bn in 2007, at the beginning of the 'Great Crash'. They then halved again, but have climbed in most years since. True, there has been no spectacular M&A boom on the scale of the pre-2000 and pre-2007 periods, but volumes have been large and reached $2,908bn in the first six months of 2018 alone. An estimate projected for the whole year of $4,400 may well turn out to be too low.[137] In any event, the value of M&As has been a reliable indicator of the emergence of capital over-accumulation, as capital seeks profitable engagement and breeds yet more capital — real and fictitious — desperate to do the same.

A 'green' Marx?

In as yet unpublished notebooks from 1868 (others were published much later as Volume III of *Capital*), Marx showed immense interest in matters of cultivation, soil exhaustion, deforestation and the physics and chemistry of agriculture. Many of his thoughts correspond to those of ecological critics of modern capitalism. Whether, in themselves, Marx's writings as a whole provide a comprehensive 'green' critique of capitalism has been a moot point among Western Marxists. Certainly, the works of Marx and — not least in his Dialectics of Nature (1873-82) — Engels provided a basis and at least a partial framework for analysing and responding to capitalism's impact on nature, the environment and planet Earth's eco-systems.[138] Thus Soviet scientists such as Sukachev and Vernadsky (in his ground-breaking book The Biosphere in 1926) developed Marxist ecological theory in the 1920s and early 1930s, which flourished alongside conservationist policies until both were eclipsed by dogmatism and the huge and vital dash for industrial growth.[139]

To begin with, Marx was acutely aware of the vital relationships between workers, production and the natural world. In Volume I of *Capital*, he noted:

> Labour is, in the first place, a process in which both man and Nature participate, and in which man of his own accord starts, regulates, and controls the material reactions between himself and Nature. He opposes himself to Nature as one of her own forces, setting in motion ... the natural forces of his body, in order to appropriate Nature's productions in a form adapted to his own wants. By thus acting on the external world and changing it, he at the same time changes his own nature.[140]

He referred to the forces of nature at work on the earth and in the water to furnish human beings with the fish, timber, fruits, minerals and other means of subsistence, which then become the subjects of human labour. From the natural world, too, come the instruments of labour: the animals whose labour power played such a major role in the earlier periods of human history; the navigable rivers, the accessible forests, the temperate climates; and the materials (stones, bones, wood, shells) which human labour fashions into tools. Marx recalled the parts played by horse and water power in the first phase of industrialisation, until humans devised more practical and effective technologies. The natural world provides the context for every mode of production, placing fetters on the productiveness of labour.[141] Nonetheless, it is human action upon nature which exploits its resources and its laws (such as those of magnetism and electricity) in order to produce for use or profit. Labour and the earth are, then, jointly the sources of society's material wealth.[142]

In the sphere of agriculture, the application of machinery, science and technology as well as seed and manure brings more land into cultivation and increases the productiveness of the soil. Capitalism had replaced the 'irrational, old-fashioned methods' of agriculture by scientific ones. Marx described, for example, how — stimulated by the final repeal of the Corn Laws (1846) — English agriculture revolutionised itself in order to compete against foreign imports of wheat: 'drainage on the most extensive scale, new methods of stall-feeding, and of the artificial cultivation of green crops, introduction of mechanical manuring apparatus, new treatment of clay soils, increased use of mineral manures, employment of the steam-engine, and of all kinds of new machinery'.[143] He believed that the soil, if properly treated, could continuously improve.[144] However, he also believed that capitalism's ruthless exploitation of the land would ultimately prove to be counter-productive because 'all progress in capitalistic agriculture is a progress in the art, not only of robbing the labourer, but of robbing the soil; all progress in increasing the fertility of the soil for a given time, is a progress towards ruining the lasting sources of that fertility'.[145]

In the sphere of industry, Marx recognised how large-scale capitalist production sought to minimise costly waste. Thus the generation and transmission of power was carried out more efficiently. In woollen and silk manufacture, machine production and — above all — in the chemicals industry, by-products were increasingly re-employed in the production process wherever possible. He also wrote about the role that good-quality machinery, tools and raw materials can play in the minimisation of such waste in the first place, which in turn relies upon the development of agriculture and the extractive and processing industries.[146] Of course, none of this negated capitalism's enormous wastefulness in other spheres:

> Capitalist production, when considered in isolation from the process of circulation and the excesses of competition, is very economical with the materialised labour objectified in commodities. Yet, more than any other mode of production, it squanders human lives, or living labour, and not only blood and flesh, but also nerve and brain.[147]

Nor was this the whole indictment. For all its progress in utilising what Marx called the 'excretions of production', capitalism had thus far failed utterly to utilise the 'excretions of consumption', namely, the 'natural waste matter discharged by the human body, remains of clothing in the form of rags', etc. Indeed, he pointed out, in London, 'they find no better use for the excretion of 4 1/2 million human beings than to contaminate the Thames with it at heavy expense'.[148]

Here was a vivid illustration of what happens when, as Marx put it in *Capital* Volume I, capitalism breaks the 'bond of union' between agriculture and manufacturing, annihilating the peasantry and collecting large centres of population in the towns. Capitalist production thereby 'disturbs the circulation of matter between man and the soil, ie., prevents the return to the soil of its elements consumed by man in the form of food and clothing; it therefore violates the conditions necessary to lasting fertility of the soil'. John Bellamy Foster refers to this as the theory of 'metabolic rift'.[149] Moreover, Marx concluded: 'Capitalist production, therefore, develops technology, and the combining together of various processes into a social whole, only by sapping the original sources of all wealth — the soil and the labourer'.[150]

In his later notebooks reproduced in Volume III, he returned to the conclusion that capitalist development will tend to ruin both nature as a source of use-value and human labour power as the source of exchange-value; in short, the two sources of society's material wealth:

> ... large landed property reduces the agricultural population to a constantly falling minimum, and confronts it with a constantly growing industrial population crowded together in large cities. It thereby creates conditions which cause an irreparable break in the coherence of social interchange prescribed by the natural laws of life. As a result, the vitality of the soil is squandered, and this prodigality is carried by commerce far beyond the borders of a particular state ... Large-scale industry and large-scale mechanised agriculture work together. If originally distinguished by the fact that the former lays waste and destroys principally labour power, hence the natural force of human beings, whereas the latter more directly exhausts and ruins the natural vitality of the soil, they join hands in the further course of development in that the industrial system in the countryside also enervates the labourers, and industry and commerce on their part supply agriculture with the means for exhausting the soil.[151]

Marx believed that accelerated development in both spheres would create the material conditions – not to say the necessity – for a 'higher synthesis' in the future, re-uniting agriculture and industry on a more advanced basis.[152] In some respects at least, it might appear as though a synthesis has already begun under state-monopoly capitalism, through the growth of agribusiness and recycling and the onset of urban sprawl. In the most developed economies, however, because these developments have proceeded on a capitalist basis, they are largely unplanned, uneven and uncoordinated, subject to the vagaries of the market. Fundamentally, humanity's interests in terms of agriculture and the natural world are contradicted by the functioning of capitalism. For instance:

> ... the dependence of the cultivation of particular agricultural products upon the fluctuations of market prices, and the continual changes in this cultivation with these price fluctuations — the whole spirit of capitalist production, which is directed toward the immediate gain of money — are in contradiction to agriculture, which has to minister to the entire range of permanent necessities of life required by the chain of successive generations. A striking illustration of this is furnished by the forests, which are only rarely managed in a way more or less corresponding to the interests of society as a whole, ie., when they are not private property, but subject to the control of the state.[153]

Today, as the 15th report of the UN Inter-Governmental Panel on Climate Change confirms, the world faces the devastating consequences of global warming. Failure to restrict the Earth's temperature rise to 1.5°C will greatly increase the economic damage, famine, disease and refugee crises caused by rising sea levels, droughts and storms. Failure to impose even the less ambitious of the 2015 Paris Agreement caps of 2°C could be catastrophic on every count. In order to achieve the lower limit and curb global greenhouse gas emissions by around 45% by 2030 on the way to net zero emissions by 2050, the thousand-plus scientists who composed or reviewed the report are calling for 'rapid and far-reaching transitions' in industry, transportation, energy, land use and construction on an 'unprecedented scale'. They propose a wide range of radical measures, including the widespread application of carbon capture technology, many of which would require extensive state intervention and public investment.[154] Whether capitalism has the capacity to counteract global warming effectively must be severely in doubt. Already, the pressure from US and German monopoly corporations to relax global warming targets is mounting, with President Trump announcing in June 2017 that the USA will withdraw from the Paris Agreement (with effect from November 2020). China, on the other hand, is on course to meet its target of no further increase in carbon emissions from 2030 and could be poised to assume the leading role in Paris process.

Perhaps only the communist mode of production is capable of the accelerated development and 'higher synthesis' of agriculture and industry, of the planet and the economy, that Marx proposed in Volume I of *Capital*.

2 The communist mode of production

Marx and the future society

There is no single, comprehensive outline in the three volumes of *Capital* of the kind of society that could or should replace capitalism. Instead, there are fragmentary glimpses.

In Volume I, Marx imagined 'a community of free individuals, carrying on their work with the means of production in common, in which the labour power of all the different individuals is consciously applied as the combined labour power of the community'. Their total product would be divided between the portion that comprises fresh means of production, which remain social, and that which comprises the means of subsistence, which are consumed individually. On what basis would the latter be distributed? Marx indicated (although it was for the sake of drawing a parallel) that the share of each individual producer would be determined by their labour time.[155] A little later in the same volume of *Capital*, he recalled his past study of the scheme of 'labour certificates' — in effect, money expressed in terms of an entitlement to the product of so many hours 'labour time' — undertaken by industrialist Robert Owen at his cooperative community in New Lanark, Scotland. Such a 'Utopian idea' could only be practicable in a community not based on commodity production, on the production of goods and services for sale at a profit.[156] This prefigures the standpoint in his *Critique of the Gotha Programme* (1875), namely, that in the period immediately following communist society's emergence from capitalism, when it is 'economically, morally and intellectually, still stamped with the birth-marks of the old society', each worker will be paid in proportion to the labour they have performed. Only in the higher phase of communist society, Marx insisted, when labour has been transformed, when the individual has developed comprehensively and the productive forces have increased so that 'all the springs of common wealth flow more abundantly', only then can communist society proclaim: 'From each according to his abilities, to each according to his needs!'[157]

In this imagined communist society, Marx proposes in Volume I of *Capital*, there would be none of the 'useless labour' and 'outrageous squandering of labour power' that characterises capitalism's 'anarchical system of competition'. Instead, labour time would be carefully planned and apportioned in accordance with society's requirements. This would not necessarily mean reducing the working day by eliminating all of the hours previously spent performing surplus labour for the capitalists. Firstly, rising living standards would require an increase in society's labour time in order to produce the increased means of subsistence now regarded as essential. Secondly, what was once 'surplus labour' (performed for the benefit of the capitalist) would become 'necessary labour' (for the benefit of society) needed to form and maintain the 'fund for reserve and accumulation'.[158] For Marx, only by increasing the intensity and productivity of labour would it become possible to shorten the working day.

In Volume I, too, he wrote in a footnote that 'in a communistic society there would be a very different scope for the employment of machinery than there can be in a bourgeois society'.[159] This is because under capitalism the introduction of labour-saving machinery might put so many people out of work, thereby cheapening the price of labour power, as to make it unnecessary if not impossible to continue doing. In any event, employing labour — especially women and children — can sometimes be cheaper than mechanisation.

In his *Economic Manuscripts of 1857-58*, Marx had drawn the contrast between the introduction of labour-saving machinery under capitalism and its introduction under communism more explicitly, pointing out that in the latter case greater productivity should mean more free time for the worker to enjoy 'leisure and higher activity'. Thus the ultimate objective should be to raise the mode of production to a higher form in which labour time and free time are not — as seen by bourgeois political economy — in conflict with one another.[160] Machines would be no longer be an alien, dominating force over living labour, but the 'property of the associated workers', the new mode of production having changed the mode of distribution of the ownership of machinery.[161]

In Volume II, Marx conceived of a communist society where there will be no money-capital, which acts as a cloak for the transactions by which capital exploits labour. Instead, society will need to 'calculate beforehand how much labour, means of production, and means of subsistence it can invest, without detriment, in such lines of business as for instance the building of railways, which do not furnish any means of production or subsistence, nor produce any useful effect for a long time, a year or more, while they extract labour, means of production and means of subsistence from the total annual production'.[162] In capitalist society, on the other hand, there is both a reluctance in the money market to provide the necessary capital and the wild speculation with borrowed money that has proved disastrous in the past. Indeed, a 'band of speculators, contractors, engineers, lawyers, etc., enrich themselves'.[163] Investment capital for other branches becomes scarce as wages initially rise along with food prices, imports and yet more speculative profiteering. It might be noted that today, most capital investment in the railway industries — even the largely privatised ones — of the most developed capitalist economies takes place under state direction and control.

In Volume I, Marx made the point that a surplus of production of Department I commodities (means of production for use in both departments) is usually desirable, not least to hold in reserve in the event of extraordinarily destructive accidents or natural disasters. 'This sort of overproduction', he maintained, 'is tantamount to control by society over the material means of its own reproduction'. However, such an excess under capitalist production is an 'evil' and an 'element of anarchy', which 'spells crisis'.[164] This echoes the *Manifesto of the Communist Party* (1848), where Marx and Engels had referred to 'an epidemic that, in all earlier epochs, would have seemed an absurdity — the epidemic of over-production'.[165] What would have been a cause for celebration in earlier types of society is a cause of crisis under capitalism!

In Volume III, Marx emphasised the importance of planning so that society's labour time is not wasted on commodities for which there is not sufficient demand for them to sell at a price approximating to their value: 'It is only where production is under the actual, predetermining control of society that the latter establishes a relation between the volume of social labour time applied in producing definite articles, and the volume of the social want to be satisfied by these articles'.[166]

In the final part of Volume III, Marx considers how capitalism creates the conditions that make possible a higher form of society. In reproducing the relations of production between the capitalist class and the working class, capitalism pumps surplus labour out of the workers, enabling a stratum of society to enjoy its idleness. This surplus value is required not only as an insurance against accidents, but also in order to expand reproduction to develop and meet the needs of a growing population. While the capitalists see this process in terms of accumulation and profit, objectively it is also 'one of the civilising aspects of capital' that it enforces surplus labour in such a way as to develop society's productive forces:

> Thus it gives rise to a stage, on the one hand, in which coercion and monopolisation of social development (including its material and intellectual advantages) by one portion of society at the expense of the other are eliminated; on the other hand, it creates the material means and embryonic conditions, making it possible in a higher form of society to combine this surplus labour with a greater reduction of time devoted to material labour in general.[167]

Marx then waxed lyrical about 'realm of freedom' made possible by the higher productivity of surplus labour in this new society with its new relations of production. Working together, the associated producers ('socialised man') would rationally regulate their relations with one another and with the forces of nature instead of being ruled by them. In conditions that are worthy of their human nature, they would produce all that is necessary, but with the least waste of human energy. On the basis of necessity, a new realm of freedom will blossom and 'the shortening of the working day is its basic prerequisite'.[168]

Three aspects of this new society can easily be overlooked because they are predominantly social in character, albeit rooted in society's economic functions. The first is that of health, safety at work, nutrition and well-being. Throughout the three volumes of *Capital*, Marx peppered his work with extracts long and short from reports into the proletariat's working and living conditions. In Volume I, he asked the question: 'What could possibly show better the character of the capitalist mode of production, than the necessity that exists for forcing upon it, by Acts of Parliament, the simplest appliances for maintaining cleanliness and health?' He points to capitalism's unwillingness and even inability to guarantee every worker 500 cubic of clean in which to breathe, citing medical authorities, the denial of which causes a range of deadly or debilitating respiratory diseases.[169]

The clear implication is that the communist mode of production would aim to meet the highest standards of workplace health and safety, sanitation and public health.

Secondly, Marx not only emphasised the value of education for all children, including paupers and factory workers, in an era before the 1870 Elementary Education Act made it compulsory throughout England and Wales (followed by Scotland in 1872); he also suggested its content in a communist society, inspired by the cooperative factory schools established by Robert Owen who 'has shown us in detail, the germ of the education of the future, an education that will, in the case of every child over a given age, combine productive labour with instruction and gymnastics, not only as one of the methods of adding to the efficiency of production, but as the only method of producing fully developed human beings'.[170]

Thirdly, there is the most profound question of the relationship between human society, its mode of production and nature. In *Capital*, Marx argued that the 'evil' of private landed property is 'a hindrance and a barrier' to the 'rational cultivation, maintenance and improvement of the soil'.[171] In fact, he believed that the higher ('differential') ground rent that landowners enjoyed at the expense of industrial and commercial capitalists — especially through licensing, royalties and the leasehold system — meant that, even under capitalism, the policy of land nationalisation could command wide support.

Only the communist mode of production would enable humanity to engage with the natural world productively and sustainably to the benefit of both society and nature. As he puts it in what became Volume III:

> Just as the savage must wrestle with Nature to satisfy his wants, to maintain and reproduce life, so must civilised man, and he must do so in all social formations and under all possible modes of production. With his development this realm of physical necessity expands as a result of his wants; but, at the same time, the forces of production which satisfy these wants also increase. Freedom in this field can only consist in socialised man, the associated producers, rationally regulating their interchange with Nature, bringing it under their common control, instead of being ruled by it as by the blind forces of Nature; and achieving this with the least expenditure of energy and under conditions most favourable to, and worthy of, their human nature.[172]

Only the common ownership of the means of production will ensure that the planet and its resources are understood to be the responsibility of all, to draw sustenance from, nurture and bequeath to humanity in the future:

> From the standpoint of a higher economic form of society, private ownership of the globe by single individuals will appear quite as absurd as private ownership of one man by another. Even a whole society, a nation, or even all simultaneously existing societies taken together, are not the owners of the globe. They are only its possessors, its usufructuaries, and, like boni patres familias ['good family fathers' — RG] they must hand it down to succeeding generations in an improved condition.[173]

In the world's first socialist state, the Soviet Union, industrialisation and the purges took a heavy toll of the environment and intellectual life, although major advances continued in forestry and climatology, Nevertheless, the Great Stalin Plan for the Transformation of Nature (1948) demonstrated how the communist mode of production can mobilise enormous resources in the shared interests of humanity and nature. Unfortunately, the restoration of unspoilt conservation and research areas ('zapovedniki') pioneered under Lenin was more than outweighed by reckless farming, forestry and irrigation policies from the mid-1950s. Fortunately, this stimulated the growth of a large and powerful environmental movement linked to a resurgence of Marxist ecological theory — all cut down by the capitalist counter-revolution of the early 1990s.[174]

The Soviet Union and the Law of Value

Thirty-four years after the death of Marx, the Great October Socialist Revolution in Russia in 1917 heralded the abolition of capitalism and a transition to socialism. Did it lead to the construction of a communist mode of production as defined, albeit only in broad outline, by Marx?

Certainly, Lenin and the ruling Communist Party claimed to have built a socialist system, using the term 'socialism' — in the style of Engels — as synonymous with the lower stage of communism, the new system which emerges from the womb of capitalism.

After the New Economic Policy was dismantled, the collectivisation of agriculture and the first Five Year Plan from 1928 effectively put an end to generalised commodity production for market sale. The central plan and its subsidiary plans decided what and how much would be produced and at what price the products would be exchanged, whether they are means of production — usually by prior contract — or means of consumption. Market demand played no independent role in determining such matters. Secondly, the means of production were almost wholly taken into social ownership by the state in the late 1920s and early 1930s. Thirdly, labour power was no longer a commodity to be bought because it produces surplus value for the capitalist. It was employed by the state, at each level, in order to perform the necessary and surplus labour deemed so essential by Marx.

That this transition from one mode of production to another was carried out in conditions which limited the possibilities for mass-scale participative democracy and workers' control, and on a basis of relative technological backwardness, does not negate the profound significance of the changes that took place. Political deficiencies in the ways in which state power was exercised can be combined with selected quotations from Marx to question whether this new system was, indeed, 'socialism'. But economically, from the standpoint of *Capital*, it most certainly was.

In particular, controversy continues around the question of whether Marx's Law of Value should or did operate in the Soviet Union. The debate ignited by Yevgeni Preobrazhensky and Nikolai Bukharin in the 1920s was later joined by Che Guevara, Ernest Mandel and others. According to this theory, commodities are exchanged in the market at prices which broadly reflect their value in terms of the average socially necessary labour time taken to produce them. This includes the surplus labour time which creates surplus value which is, as Marx put it in *Capital* Volume III, the 'immediate purpose and compelling motive of capitalist production'.[175] This is the basis on which decisions about employment, investment and production are taken under capitalism.

Stalin pointed out that this Law of Value operated only to a strictly limited extent in the Soviet Union, tightly constrained by the small size of commodity production for the market — chiefly of commodities for personal consumption — and the absence of private ownership of the means of production. In Department I (producer goods), while the Law of Value was taken into account when it came to production costs, accounting, profitability and pricing, it did not perform a regulatory role.[176] The key decisions about the allocation and deployment of resources, wages, prices and net revenue (or profit) margins were set by the state planning authorities, in accordance with the social, economic and political (not least the military) priorities decided by the Communist Party of the Soviet Union (CPSU).

Almost all prices were fixed or capped — for 5-15 year periods in the case of the capital goods sector (Department I) — irrespective of changes in cost, supply or demand. While differential pricing between industrial and agricultural products eased after the 1930s, it persisted until at least the agricultural price hikes of 1953-54, while almost one-quarter of all collective farms still needed state-subsidised life-support in the mid-1960s. Levels of turnover tax and state subsidy also helped determine most price levels, with the former frequently varied in an effort to match retail sales to the plans. Following Prime Minister Kosygin's economic reforms announced in 1965, capital charges on assets were introduced and prices of most primary industrial products (oil, iron ore, coal, metals and timber) rose sharply. All this meant that most prices bore little relation to labour-time values.[177]

In the socialist economies of Eastern Europe, the so-called 'socialist calculation debate' also shifted from the realm of theoretical controversy in the 1920s and 1930s to that of practical policy from 1948. In Poland, notably, economist and government adviser Oskar Lange wrote extensively about the challenges of applying market mechanisms in a centrally planned economy, especially in relation to prices, interest rates and resource allocation.

Here is not the place for a detailed assessment of the performance, strengths and weaknesses of the Soviet Union's economy or those of the socialist states of Eastern Europe (which differed substantially from one another in structure and policies). But it was the case that Soviet growth rates were generally higher than those of the USA and Western Europe from 1950 until the end of the 1960s; Eastern Europe decreasingly so. Soviet growth then became more erratic during the 1970s, falling behind the USA, France and — albeit narrowly — West Germany, although not behind Britain. The socialist economies of Eastern Europe actually grew faster during the 1970s than those of France, West Germany, Britain, the USA and even Italy (although not Japan). In the decade before the collapse and counter-revolution began in 1989, the Soviet economy was outstripping Western Europe until 1984, while Eastern Europe held its own until 1987 before dipping steeply into recession, soon followed by the Soviet Union:

GDP % growth in each decade [178]

	1950-59	1960-69	1970-79	1980-89
Soviet Union	60.0	48.9	26.3	19.2
Eastern Europe	55.1	47.7	44.4	6.2
France	46.0	62.6	35.5	22.9
West Germany	94.8	44.2	29.6	17.8
Italy	70.8	71.7	37.5	22.1
Britain	23.2	29.2	23.6	29.2
USA	37.2	50.3	37.2	34.8
Japan	106.0	144.1	50.1	40.8

Of course, in any international comparisons it should be borne in mind that the Soviets were measuring mostly tangible output and closely related services, with no significant 'output' from financial, commercial and property services. If we consider industrial production alone, for example, the Soviet Union's share of world output rose steadily from 4.9% in 1938 to 11.1% in 1966 and 14.2% in 1979, before levelling off; over the post-war period between 1948 and 1979, the US share fell by more than a third, Britain's halved while the rest of Western Europe remained more or less constant.[179]

Since the counter-revolution in the Soviet Union and the other socialist countries, an expanding literature has developed claiming to show that Soviet — and even CIA — accounts of their economic performance were grossly exaggerated in the course of the 20th century, that the statistics were false by accident or design, etc. But while the socialist states and governments are no longer around to defend themselves, there are trenchant (and non-socialist) critics of this often ideologically motivated revisionism.[180]

More instructive have been the differing analyses of the reasons for the deteriorating performance of the Soviet economy by the 1970s and early 1980s. These have identified some key factors, including: weaknesses and failures in resource allocation during different periods (eg., too much investment in primary industry instead of meeting the under-estimated demand for consumer goods; too much investment in military and related R&D and production); a pricing system that allowed poor productivity, low quality, waste and inflation to go undetected and uncorrected by higher planning authorities; inadequate systems to measure consumer demand and satisfaction; inadequate or non-existent incentives to encourage more efficient deployment of productive factors (machinery, labour power, technology) and therefore higher productivity; the declining supply of urban labour power; and the long-term impact of failures in designing, correcting or renewing strategic reforms and plans (whether the hit-and-miss zig-zags of the Khrushchev era or the unsustained

Kosygin programme of 1965-71).[181] Undoubtedly, the cumulative effect of underlying weaknesses and problems, which worsened in the 1960s and 1970s, created the conditions in which by the late 1980s many people either were not prepared to defend the socialist system or actively supported its dissolution. While there were other causes of dissatisfaction and hostility, in some cases these were exacerbated by economic failure.

Clearly, a more advanced system of socialist democracy in which workers, citizens and their collective organisations have more opportunities to raise, discuss and formulate the responses to economic problems, on the basis of full and proper disclosure of information, would have improved economic performance. The same is true of other aspects of society. Yet this is not the same as asserting that the socialist economic basis of the Soviet and Eastern European societies was fundamentally flawed and even doomed from the outset. On the contrary, the socialist economies produced spectacular results during most of their existence, in the face of powerful imperialist hostility, attempted counter-revolution and — for the eastern Soviet Union, Poland, Hungary and East Germany in particular — amid the wreckage of a catastrophic war. In addition, the COMECON states extended substantial aid to many Third World countries and national liberation movements, as well as rebuilding the cities of North Korea obliterated by US bombing in the early 1950s and helping Cuba and Vietnam survive international blockades organised by US imperialism.

In fact, the final blows that plunged the Soviet economy into near-collapse were delivered not by socialist policies but by pro-capitalist ones. Although there was an intermittent slowdown in the growth of production and investment in the early 1980s (and at best a flat-lining of agricultural output), with the war in Afghanistan taking an increasing toll on resources, the economy was not in crisis as defined in capitalist economies. President Gorbachev's initial perestroika reforms addressed some — but by no means all — of the deeper weaknesses and problems in the Soviet economic system. However, before they could take full effect they were hit by a damaging fall in oil prices in 1986 and then transformed by series of policies announced in 1987 and 1988 which undermined centralised planning and public ownership and facilitated the rise of markets, competition and private enterprise — not least through the promotion of cooperatives that were, in substance according to Hanson (2003), more akin to 'capitalist partnerships'. Central planning and disciplined budgeting were dismantled as anarchy in production and the public finances gained ground. At the same time, the onset of glasnost (roughly, 'openness') had spawned an ideological struggle against Communism and aspects of the Soviet system which the Communist Party of the Soviet Union was by this time incapable of fighting effectively.

The resulting chaos stimulated the anti-Communist Party, anti-Soviet, nationalist and separatist tendencies that unleashed full-scale counter-revolution in 1991. This, in turn, sent the economy into a tailspin which culminated in financial chaos, the break-up of the Soviet Union, wholesale privatisation, depression, mass unemployment and poverty and the biggest peacetime fall in life expectancy in recorded history.

Socialism or 'state capitalism'?

Planning and managing the Soviet Union's vast, interconnected, expanding economy proved to be an enormous, complex task. Problems of resource allocation, capital accumulation, investment, productivity and incentive recurred in different forms despite an often bewildering array of mechanisms and initiatives.

Furthermore, the transformation of surplus labour into fresh and additional means of production had to be a transparent process, undisguised by prices and the wages system. A combination of consent and coercion by various means was regarded as necessary on the part of the CPSU, the state, managers and even the trades unions.

This provided the pretext for sections of the left in the imperialist countries to abandon the often difficult responsibility of defending — however critically — the Soviet Union and the socialist states against an enormous, relentless anti-communist, anti-Soviet offensive. Whether in the adventurous, idealist traditions of Trotsky or Mao, some theorists developed an analysis that characterised the Soviet Union not as a society building socialism, but as a 'deformed' or 'degenerate' workers' state, stuck in some transitional limbo between capitalism and socialism. Insofar as these critiques are solely or primarily concerned with the exercise of state power, they fall outside the scope of this book.

However, the theory which characterised the Soviet system as one of 'state capitalism' claims to be based on Marxist political economy in general, and *Capital* in particular, and so merits some attention. Whether in its semi-Trotskyist, Maoist or anarchist manifestations, this theory holds that the CPSU leadership and its apparatchiks took the place of the capitalist class in exploiting the labour power of the working class. A new bureaucratic ruling class or elite commanded the means of production and used its political power to maximise the extraction of surplus labour and surplus value from the working class in accordance with capitalist imperatives, not least the accumulation of capital.

Although he was not the first to make a case for the 'state capitalism' theory on ostensibly Marxist grounds, Tony Cliff's 1948 article reworked as *State Capitalism in Russia* (1955 and 1974) has had the biggest impact over time, at least in Britain.[182] In it, Cliff portrayed the workers in Soviet Russia as defenceless, atomised, set against each other (by Nazi-style piece-work!), subordinate from 1928 to the means of production and to capital accumulation (through 'unprecedented brutality'), and poverty-stricken despite leaps in labour productivity. He dealt mostly in workers' net wages and largely discounted the growing and substantial 'social wage' paid through free and universal healthcare, education, housing, transport and other services provided to the Russian people for the first time in their history. He pointed out that the armaments industry occupied a decisive place in Russia's economic system — although it's not clear whether or to what extent Cliff approved of the Soviet state's efforts to protect itself from capitalist fascism and imperialism in the run-up to World War Two. His contention that a 'Stalinist bureaucracy' carried out a counter-revolution in 1928, and that this 'political expropriation of the working class is thus identical with its economic expropriation', rests on a bed of the purest sophistry, dragging Adam

Smith, James Burnham and Nazi Germany (again!) into spurious comparisons. For Cliff, the 'division of the total product of society among the different classes' not only persisted or, rather, was restored in the Soviet Union, based on the Marxist Law of Value: state monopoly ownership of the means of production, together with exploitation of the workers, also meant that dependence on that law had assumed its 'purest, most direct and absolute form' in Stalin's Russia. (It should be noted that this was a counter-revolution of which most Communists, socialists, workers and capitalists around the world in 1928 were entirely unaware).

Undaunted, Cliff pressed on to argue that the Stalinist bureaucracy was a class which represented 'the extreme and pure personification of capital', although the party and state officials had no entitlements to possess or pass on any economic assets at all. But they could bequeath their 'connections', Cliff pointed out with breathtaking feebleness. Those who wielded political power and economic control in the Soviet system may have been able to divert and transform a very small portion of society's surplus labour into their own extra personal consumption, but this was an insignificant factor in economic decision-making and produced nothing like the levels of social inequality in capitalist society.

Cliff's divorce from the key concepts of *Capital* was complete when he dealt with the Law of Value in detail (in Chapter 7). There, he jumbled up and then re-labelled three distinct concepts: (1) 'state capitalism' as understood by Lenin, namely, direct state intervention in the capitalist economy through procurement, regulation or nationalisation; (2) 'state-monopoly capitalism', which Lenin defined as the fusion of the political power of the state with the economic power of the capitalist monopolies, as happened in the Great Imperialist War, and which he characterised as the 'complete material preparation for socialism, the threshold of socialism, a rung on the ladder of history between which and the rung called socialism there are no intermediate rungs'; [183] and (3) monopoly state ownership of society's means of production — what Lenin, along with Marx and Engels, would have recognised as the economic basis for the lower stage of communism, namely, socialism. Cliff uses the term in (2) to characterise a capitalist war economy (although militarism and war accelerate the development of state-monopoly capitalism rather than define what is a new stage of capitalism). He uses the term in (1) to characterise the mode of production outlined in (3), although they are separated by the Russian wall of a revolution, the transfer of state power from one class to another and the subsequent, near total, expropriation of the capitalist class.

Even more absurdly, in his desperation to claim that the Marxist Law of Value continued to operate more or less fully in the Soviet Union, Cliff drew a nonsensical analogy:

> The Stalinist state is in the same position vis-à-vis the total labour time of Russian society as a factory owner vis-à-vis the labour of his employees. In other words, the division of labour is planned. But what is it that determines the actual division of total labour time in Russian society? If Russia had not to compete

with other countries, this division would be absolutely arbitrary. But as it is, Stalinist decisions are based on factors outside of control, namely the world economy, world competition. From this point of view the Russian state is in a similar position to the owner of a single capitalist enterprise competing with other enterprises.

The rate of exploitation, that is, the ratio between surplus value and wages (s/v) does not depend on the arbitrary will of the Stalinist government, but is dictated by world capitalism.

The notion that the CPSU leadership (or the 'Stalinist' state or bureaucracy) was in the same position as a factory owner is, of course, ludicrous. The Soviet economy was not one giant aggregated factory competing in a global capitalist market against rival capitalists, and thereby subject to the imperatives of capitalist accumulation, producing commodities for their exchange-value in order to maximise surplus value, all basically in accordance with Marx's Law of Value. More than 90% of Soviet production was for home consumption, only half and often less than that was for any kind of market, and that was usually a market from which non-Soviet goods were excluded. The notion that Soviet domestic pricing policy was influenced by — let alone subject to — international capitalist market prices, for example, is not supported by any serious study. While it was the case, after the 1958 Bucharest Agreement, that trade between the Council for Mutual Economic Assistance (COMECON) countries was based on such prices, these were varied substantially through bilateral contracts. In any event, neither intra-COMECON nor wider international trade comprised more than a small proportion of Soviet economic activity (much less than 5% in total until the 1970s). Even towards the end, total foreign trade never accounted for more than 8% of Soviet GNP, and much of that was with other COMECON members or Third World countries on a non-competitive basis.

As though in recognition of his own theoretical confusion, Cliff also tried to explain how a system that was 'really in permanent crisis' could conceal its true condition behind a mask of more or less permanent growth (albeit with cyclical slowdowns) and full employment. It could do so, he insisted, because it was in fact a 'war economy' which occupied the opposite pole to socialism. This enabled the Stalinist bureaucracy to narrow the economic gap with the Western powers by pursuing an 'imperialist policy' of expansion in order to 'loot capital' and exploit the labour and natural resources of the Ukraine, the Caucuses, Rumania, Bulgaria, Manchuria, etc., just as Japanese imperialism and Nazi Germany had done before.

Apart from being an odd way to characterise post-war reparations and the necessity for the Soviet state to defend itself against unremitting imperialist hostility, this utterly misrepresented COMECON arrangements — which helped the east European economies to catch up with Soviet growth rates in the 1960s before overtaking them in the 1970s — and Soviet aid and solidarity policies. It also disregarded the negative impact of high military spending on civilian technology and investment, productivity and on the production of consumer goods. The CPSU leadership always regarded its defence preparations as a regrettable but necessary burden, rather than the means by which it could 'loot' Russia's neighbours.

Cliff's work demonstrates how, in just about every single respect, state-capitalist theory failed to correspond to reality in the Soviet and other socialist COMECON economies, still less explain it. Charles Bettelheim's three-volume Maoist analysis *Class Struggles in the USSR* (1974-82), now popular in some anarchist circles, likewise paid little attention to concrete realities and developments in the Soviet Union. Bettelheim philosophised tortuously against what he misnamed the 'economism' of the CPSU leadership — or, rather, of a largely undefined 'state bourgeoisie' — with its emphasis on public ownership of the means of production, the development of the forces of production (especially technology) and the capacity of both to transform the state, the working class and the peasantry in the direction of socialism. His work adds almost nothing to our knowledge or understanding of how the Soviet economy was organised, containing no new research to accompany its turgid, tendentious and superficial analysis.

In the Soviet Union and other fledgeling socialist economies, most goods were produced for their use-value in the manner anticipated by Marx. Although, from time to time, the labour-value of each product was calculated as an aid to accountancy and more efficient resource allocation and production, goods were not produced because they had an exchange-value arising from the exploitation of labour power. Under capitalism, on the other hand, which goods will be produced and in what quantities is determined by their exchange-value as commodities for sale in the market, where their surplus value can be realised. Of course, Marx noted in *Capital* Volume I, the capitalist will be praised as a 'moral citizen' whose sole concern is to produce goods for their use-value, for the benefit of society and the people in it. But the real motive is to make a profit and re-invest much of it, with the intention of expanding its value.

> use-values must therefore never be looked upon as the real aim of the capitalist; neither must the profit on any single transaction. The restless never-ending process of profit-making alone is what he aims at. This boundless greed after riches, this passionate chase after exchange-value, is common to the capitalist and the miser; but while the miser is merely a capitalist gone mad, the capitalist is a rational miser. The never-ending augmentation of exchange-value, which the miser strives after, by seeking to save his money from circulation, is attained by the more acute capitalist, by constantly throwing it afresh into circulation.[184]

This production of exchange-values rather than use-values, in a system of generalised commodity production, is an essential feature of any kind of capitalism. So, it might be thought, is the presence of a class of capitalists who command the generalised production of commodities for their exchange-value. None of this was the case in the Soviet Union.

'Socialism with Chinese characteristics'

Many of those on the far left who regard the former Soviet Union as 'state capitalist' also analyse the People's Republic of China and its economic basis in the same way, reaching the same conclusions. Indeed, they may believe that this characterisation has been amply borne out by the developments of recent decades. Interestingly, some champions of capitalism are equally keen to claim China's extraordinary economic and social advances for capitalism or — at the very least — for 'state capitalism'.

The questions therefore arise: is China's economy socialist? Has it ever been? Within a short time of the 1949 revolution, most industry and commerce in the cities and large towns had been nationalised and production was directed by the first Five Year Plan (1953-57). In what was largely a rural, semi-feudal society, the landowners were expropriated and agricultural and handicraft production taken over by village communes. Previously subjected to spectacular fits and starts, the process of industrialisation and technological progress accelerated enormously as a result of the 'Reform and Opening Up' strategy adopted in 1978 by the Communist Party of China (CPC) led by Deng Xiaoping. Non-mainland Chinese and foreign capital was invited to establish enterprises in special coastal zones and has come to play a significant part in China's domestic economy, as major sources of advanced technology as well as investment and employment.

In this respect, China's model for rapid development broke fundamentally from the one implemented in the Soviet Union during the Stalin period — the model, indeed, which the CPC itself attempted to replicate in the substantially different socio-economic and political conditions of China, ultimately with near disastrous consequences. Instead, the CPC has designed its own model better suited to China's objective conditions and the aspirations of its people, albeit one bearing striking similarities to Lenin's New Economic Policy.

Additionally, the CPC has chosen to engage with capitalist globalisation on its own terms, as far as is possible, rather than pursue a policy based on autarky. This has meant not only permitting the growth of limited private economic ownership and markets, but enthusiastically participating in international trade and investment.

Internally, since the further restructuring and consolidation reforms of 1993, state ownership has become concentrated in large enterprises with monopoly control retained in key sectors such as energy, transport, communications, armaments and finance. Today, according to official statistics, what might be called the socialised sector (viz. enterprises designated as state- or collective-owned, cooperative, 'joint ownership' and 'state sole funded') account for 15% of all assets and 8% of revenues in China's domestic industrial economy, whereas private enterprises claimed 42% and 57%, respectively. But two other categories — limited liability corporations (LLCs) and non-private share-holding corporations (SHCs) — control the balance of 43% of assets and 35% of revenues. These LLCs and SHCs are economic units with a mix of individual, private corporate and socialised sector investors or shareholders. The socialised interest is usually predominant, not least because of the powerful role played by the State Asset Supervision and Administration Commission (SASAC), which actively represents state shareholdings in all non-state enterprises to make sure that wider economic, social and environmental goals are fully taken into account. In effect, this means that around half of industry in China remains either socially owned or directly state-controlled. If we strip out non-Chinese owned companies, which account for 12% of assets and 13% of revenues, the socialised and state-controlled enterprises account for two-thirds of assets and half of all revenues.[185]

In the countryside, extensive reforms have transferred the larger share of agricultural and handicraft production, together with land-lease rights on the basis of social ownership, from village communes to households.

Various mechanisms are used — state ownership and shareholdings, state credit, direction of private investment, public sector contracts, licensing conditions for foreign TNCs, etc. — to ensure that all major economic operations assist or conform to the requirements of state policy and, in particular, the Five Year Plan. The current Thirteenth Plan (2016-20), like other most recent ones, sets out the main domestic priorities: economic growth in a small number of metropolitan centres and across China's much poorer interior; the rapid spread of transport and communications links; the application of ecological principles and goals to all economic and social policies, not least in terms of energy efficiency and sustainability; more emphasis on efficient investment, bigger company surpluses, consumer-led production, higher wages and the ongoing alleviation of poverty; and all this on the basis of a long-term, constant, coordinated, innovation-driven and 'medium-high'— very high by Western capitalist standards — level of growth in GDP.[186]

Beyond China, account must also be taken of the TNCs from mainland China that have made such a dramatic entry onto the globalisation stage. According to the Fortune Global 500 list, 98 of the world's biggest 500 TNCs in 2014 were Chinese (only the US has a larger number). Of these, no fewer than three-quarters (76) are state-owned, including the top twelve.[187]

The CPC characterises its developmental model as a 'socialist market economy' in which strategic public ownership and Communist Party rule are the decisive factors. The new General Programme of the CPC declares: 'China is currently in the primary stage of socialism and will remain so for a long time to come. This is a stage of history that cannot be bypassed as China, which used to be economically and culturally lagging, makes progress in socialist modernization; it will take over a century'.[188]

The world's foremost imperialist state — the USA — broadly agrees with this assessment. Indeed, this is the basis of the case made by US representatives in July 2018 for China's exclusion from the World Trade Organisation.[189] Their submission accuses China of fundamentally breaching the 'free market', free trade principles of WTO membership, complaining that: 'At its core, the framework of China's economy is set by the Chinese government and the Chinese Communist Party, which exercise control directly and indirectly over the allocation of resources through instruments such as government ownership and control of key economic actors and government directives ... The government and the CPC permit market forces to operate only to the extent that such activity accords with the objectives of national economic and industrial policy'. It's as though the latter were a bad thing!

In particular, the US officials point to the specific features of China's economy which define it as socialist rather than capitalist: centralised planning, dominant and statutory state ownership in key sectors (eg., banking, energy, transport, telecommunications, health, education), one or other form of social ownership of almost all land, no internal free market in labour, the supremacy in law of Communist Party rule and the role of CP organisation in private sector workplaces.

Of course, China's socialist trajectory is not without hazards, risks and its own contradictions. Immediately after 1949, Chinese society faced the contradictions between its low-level, largely pre-capitalist forces of production and the Communist Party's aspirations for a society based on post-capitalist relations of production. There was little or nothing in Marx's *Capital* by way of theoretical guidance to help resolve those contradictions. The CPC had to proceed by trial, error and innovation. Today, its General Programme identifies the 'principal contradiction' in Chinese society as that 'between the ever-growing needs of the people for a better life and unbalanced and inadequate development'. Within this, as Chinese society's productive forces continue to grow rapidly and production relations have been transformed, a new and higher set of contradictions also arise: between the new Chinese capitalists and a new urban and industrial working class; between markets and centralised planning; and between Communist Party rule and narrow, 'economistic' perceptions of class interest within the capitalist and working classes. Naturally, these contradictions find some reflection within the CPC itself, as well as in the Chinese mass media and other aspects of society.

But before socialists and communists outside China rush to advice and judgement, they should study China and its recent history with some rigour, while also reflecting upon their own record when it comes to making revolutions and building socialism.[190]

Cooperation and cooperatives

Marx attached great significance to the role that combined, social labour plays in the development of capitalism's productive forces, helping to create the conditions and lay the foundations for the new, communist mode of production. How could or should workers, freed from capitalist relations of production, continue to work in association with one another in the new sets of relations?

It is unfortunate that many would-be followers of Marx have allowed his critique of 'utopian socialism' in the *Manifesto of the Communist Party* (1848) to lead them to ignore or undervalue his subsequent remarks about producers' and consumers' cooperatives.

For instance, in a note in Volume I of *Capital*, Marx refers to Robert Owen's cooperative factories and stores as 'isolated elements of transformation'; they demonstrated how significant elements of capitalist production and exchange can be transformed. They were 'isolated' in the sense that they were separate from the working class movement, which alone could and would lead the struggle to overcome the capitalist mode of production. This last point was something, Marx believed, that Owen but not his followers had come to understand.[191] That is why, in an earlier footnote, he had referred to cooperatives 'being used as a cloak for reactionary humbug', presumably by cooperators or capitalism's apologists.[192]

In Volume III, Marx points out that just as capitalist owners in their joint stock companies no longer directly supervise production themselves, hiring managers instead, so 'Cooperative factories furnish proof that the capitalist has become no less redundant as a functionary in production as he himself, looking down from his high perch, finds the big landowner redundant'. Marx went on to argue that 'in a cooperative factory the antagonistic nature of the labour of supervision disappears, because the manager is paid by the labourers instead of representing capital counterposed to them ... the capitalist disappears as superfluous from the production process'.[193] Thus both cooperatives and joint stock companies exposed the reality that the capitalists' wealth does not accrue from any work they might do in the production process, but from the profit and interest derived from surplus value created by the workers.

At the same time, whereas cooperatives demonstrate that enterprises can thrive without any necessity for private capitalist ownership, they also have to participate in — and thereby help perpetuate — a capitalist market economy. Subject to that economy's rules and pressures, their own collectivist outlook may go no further than the enterprise and its local community, while other enterprises are unavoidably regarded and treated as competitors.

The Mondragon Cooperative Corporation (MCC) in Euzkadi, the Spanish Basque country, exhibits the contradictions of cooperatives in a capitalist society on an extensive scale. Established in 1956, it comprises 250 enterprises employing 74,000 workers (around half of them cooperative members) in the manufacturing, retail, financial and technology sectors. The MCC has weathered recessions more successfully than many of its capitalist competitors. When its main domestic appliances producer, Fagor Electrodomésticos, failed in 2013, all but 300 of the 1,700 workforce took voluntary retirement or found work in other co-ops. In recent years, the MCC has forged international relationships and now has 125 production subsidiaries in China, India, USA, Mexico and Brazil which account for almost three-quarters of the federation's sales. It also participates in more than 30 R&D projects elsewhere in Europe.[194]

Yet Mondragon has its negative features. During the Fagor crisis and at other times, while the cooperative members are protected, the same does not apply to the 35,000 or so non-member contract workers and employees — many of them temporary — in MCC subsidiaries. As Kasmir (1996) reveals, levels of member participation in key decision-making are low, there is a significant degree of misunderstanding and even antagonism between workers and management (despite far lower income differentials than in a typical capitalist enterprise) and between members and non-members. The extent of solidarity with workers outside the locality is lower than in neighbouring towns, as is involvement in left-wing political activity (Mondragon was until recently a bastion of support for the right-of-centre Basque National Party).[195] Out of the internal conflicts of recent years, which have included strikes and occupations against cooperative managers, initiatives have arisen to build trade unions within the corporation.

Efforts to reconcile cooperatism and trade unionism have also produced some interesting developments elsewhere, in Latin America and France, where unions have involved themselves in rescuing threatened enterprises and turned them into cooperatives governed by a unionised workforce. The United Steelworkers of the USA and Canada have been working with Mondragon to develop a unionised cooperative model for workers' buyouts of failing companies.[196]

Nonetheless, the history of cooperatives in general indicates that in themselves, shorn of any political or ideological orientation, they are unlikely to play any significant role in the struggle to overthrow capitalist state power so that a new communist, cooperative mode of production can be built. Under capitalism, cooperatives have to function, compete and survive in a market economy dominated by monopolies. They have to adapt to that economy's laws and tendencies, including at least to some extent to its outlook. This contradiction between social ownership and competition cannot be resolved on the basis of capitalism. The resolution may lie in a socialist planned economy, although even then there would be contradictions to be overcome: between collective planning at national, regional and local levels on the one hand and cooperative autonomy on the other; between the goal of full employment and the freedom of cooperatives to retrench, lay off workers or go into voluntary liquidation; and between the collectivist outlook of a politicised working class and more localised interests, preferences and objectives.

Notwithstanding their difficulties and limitations, Marx saw in workers' cooperatives glimpses of the future mode of production, in which cooperative labour could continue and flourish without capitalist ownership:

> The cooperative factories of the labourers themselves represent within the old form the first sprouts of the new, although they naturally reproduce, and must reproduce, everywhere in their actual organisation all the shortcomings of the prevailing system. But the antithesis between capital and labour is overcome within them, if at first only by way of making the associated labourers into their own capitalist, ie., by enabling them to use the means of production for the employment of their own labour. They show how a new mode of production naturally grows out of an old one, when the development of the material forces of production and of the corresponding forms of social production have reached a particular stage. Without the factory system arising out of the capitalist mode of production there could have been no cooperative factories. Nor could these have developed without the credit system arising out of the same mode of production. The credit system is not only the principal basis for the gradual transformation of capitalist private enterprises into capitalist stock companies, but equally offers the means for the gradual extension of cooperative enterprises on a more or less national scale.[197]

Later, Engels in *Socialism: Utopian and Scientific* (1880) paid fulsome tribute to many of Owen's ideas and activities, making very specific points about cooperatives (and labour tokens):

> He introduced as transition measures to the complete communistic organisation of society, on the one hand, co-operative societies for retail trade and production. These have since that time, at least, given practical proof that the merchant and the manufacturer are socially quite unnecessary. On the other hand, he introduced labour bazaars for the exchange of the products of labour through the medium of labour-notes, whose unit was a single hour of work; institutions necessarily doomed to failure, but completely anticipating Proudhon's bank of exchange of a much later period, and differing entirely from this in that it did not claim to be the panacea for all social ills, but only a first step towards a much more radical revolution of society.[198]

Lenin, too, grasped the potential value of cooperatives in the transition to socialism once state power had been achieved. They were no longer the stuff of 'ridiculously fantastic' dreams of those who saw them as an alternative to the revolutionary class struggle for political power. Now near the end of his life, in 1923, he believed that state power, state control of all large-scale means of production and state supervision of private enterprise would be all that is needed to 'build a complete socialist society out of cooperatives, out of cooperatives alone'.[199]

Although Lenin emphasised the need to enrol the mass of the peasantry into cooperatives, the collectivisation of agriculture from 1928 drew them into collective and state farms where they had little or no control of the enterprise. Land remained nationalised in Soviet Russia under the 1917 decree. Industrial cooperatives began to multiply in the mid-1920s, but they too were incorporated into the First Five Year Plan (1928-32) and its command system. While this substantially limited their autonomy, they were used to enrol private artisans. Even so, their membership across the Soviet Union never rose much above 2% of the total workforce and they were used extensively as a source of skilled labour for the state sector of industry.[200] Consumer cooperatives became part of the system of state stores in 1935, while remaining the predominant means of retail distribution in the countryside.

In most countries of Eastern Europe, except Albania, cooperatives had risen to economic prominence in the period up to the Second World War, notably in agriculture. This also meant that, with the exception of Poland, authoritarian right-wing governments went to considerable lengths in efforts to control, corrupt or co-opt them.

In pre-war Czechoslovakia, there were more than 11,500 agricultural cooperatives including many involved in savings and credit, processing and manufacturing. After the 1948 revolution, the Unified Agricultural Cooperatives Act (1949) collectivised most of the land and, over the following 20 years, farm productivity caught up with the developed capitalist economies. Czechoslovakia's dependency on food imports was brought to an end. In just five years, between 1954 and 1959, agricultural cooperative workers went from being 6% of the national workforce to 14%, while non-agricultural cooperative workers almost doubled to 2%.[201] However, until the early 1970s, the main beneficiaries of surplus labour in the countryside were the urban industrial workers and intelligentsia. By the 1980s, this transfer had been halted and the vast majority of agricultural workers (more than 70%) were employed in cooperatives, with only 15% on state farms and the remainder on private farms. Despite the inefficiencies of Czech agriculture's socialist system — notably its lack of incentives and heavy reliance on state subsidies — many cooperative members have resisted attempts by capitalist governments since the 1990s to abandon their cooperatives for the revived private sector.

The same is the case in Hungary, where cooperative farmers received extensive specialist education and technological assistance from the socialist state, while mostly working a standard 8-hour day over a 5-day week. Hungary's cooperative farms also enjoyed a large degree of autonomy under state control from the 1950s onwards.[202] In Bulgaria, Communist-led state policy after 1944 was to encourage all agricultural cooperatives and, after the collectivisation of land use in 1949, award them an increasing share of arable land. In the absence of state farms, agricultural 'labour cooperatives' grew in number from 382 in 1945 to 3,290 by 1958, occupying 93% of arable land. Then they were amalgamated in 1959 and, losing much of their autonomy, were turned into agro-industrial businesses in 1970, as the cooperators became waged employees.[203]

Housing cooperatives in Bulgaria accounted for more than one-third of house construction until the mid-1970s, when the state sector expanded rapidly before declining to previous levels in the 1980s. In war-torn Czechoslovakia, on the other hand, housing cooperatives were largely incorporated into the state sector in all but name, where the emphasis was on the quantity rather than the quality of new building. In Poland, where wartime destruction was greatest, new forms of housing cooperatives were established by the socialist state power and given the central role in construction and management, supported by new savings, credit and social land ownership systems. By 1980, housing cooperatives accounted for 80% of house-building, while also collaborating with local authorities in the construction of many other community facilities. The whole system was abolished in 1990 as incompatible with the capitalist market.[204]

In the German Democratic Republic, the Workers' Housing Cooperatives Law (1954) led to workplace-based housing cooperatives producing between a third and a half of all new dwellings in the early 1960s and the 1970s. However, coop members played a minimal role in policy-making, management and governance, while far-reaching reforms were aborted by counter-revolution in the early 1990s.[205] Artisan cooperatives were promoted in place of private self-employment to the extent that these were providing 36% of such services by 1962 — up from less than 2% just five years earlier. Such cooperatives producing industrial goods were nationalised in 1972.[206] Cooperative farms with their legal entitlement to land ownership were promoted as part of the post-war land expropriation programme, although these were increasingly absorbed into the state system from the 1960s.

In Yugoslavia, the socialist mode of production was characterised by the predominance of workers' self-managed enterprises within a state-controlled market economy. This allowed workers extensive control over the production, management and distribution of their own surplus value. On the negative side, however, it perpetuated at least some of the insecurity and crises of a competitive, capitalist economy while also exacerbating inequalities of income and wealth between the workforces, local communities, regions and nations of the Yugoslav federation. The decline and degeneration of centralised Communist Party political control helped create the basis for implosion and a calamitous civil war in the 1990s.

Marketisation, privatisation, the restitution of property to pre-socialist owners have, together with an end to state support, destroyed large swathes of the cooperative systems, particularly in artisan services and industry, and especially in Czechoslovakia and the GDR. While some capitalist regimes are attempting to revive their cooperative sectors, this is being done on a different economic, political and ideological basis.

At the same time, socialist experiments in cooperatism not only continue but are being reinvigorated in Cuba and China.

In the former, the cooperative farms that have existed since the 1959 revolution are now at the cutting edge of sustainable organic agriculture, producing a wide range of crops. Together with the innovations in state-backed urban farming, they have replaced Cuba's previous dependency on sugar exports to the Soviet Union. The recent economic liberalisation measures under President Raoul Castro have included not only licensing small-scale private enterprise, but also transforming hundreds of state-run services into democratic workers' cooperatives, owned and run by their members. While high levels of worker and consumer satisfaction are reported, the Cuban government has also found it necessary to combat a new problem — corporate tax evasion.

In China, the 1950 Law on Cooperatives combined with tax and state credit assistance hugely expanded the number of farming and marketing cooperatives to 19,000 by 1957. They accounted for one-quarter of agricultural production. But they were then converted into state farms. Since the 1978 reforms, however, rural Supply and Marketing Cooperatives (SMCs) have been re-established and incubated with a range of state supports and incentives. Federated together, they account for significant proportions of China's farm machinery, fertilizer, cotton, recycling and food production industries.[207] In addition, there are also thriving state-backed handicraft cooperatives and, embracing 200m households, a vast network of rural credit unions.

Thus, today as in the past, socialist construction is throwing up a rich variety of initiatives and experiences in relation to workers' and consumers' cooperatives. The same can be said about the many examples of such cooperatives that operate in developed capitalist societies, including in Britain. For instance, the miners of Tower Colliery in Hirwaun, Wales, used their redundancy pay and a short-term bank loan from the Cooperative Bank to buy their mine from the National Coal Board in 1995. They had been told that their operations were uneconomic in current market conditions, with near inaccessible reserves and disappearing markets. The cooperative membership appointed their militant former National Union of Mineworkers lodge secretary as chair of the management board and the former lodge chair as personnel officer, hired other managers and consultants, found new markets for the coal, enjoyed large pay rises and generous pensions and invested a major share of the cooperative's profits in local community economic, social and cultural projects. The colliery closed 13 years later, once the accessible reserves were exhausted.

While there were tensions and contradictions between the managers, on the one side, and the miners as cooperative members and employees on the other, the enterprise vividly demonstrated that neither workers nor their enterprises need capitalists in any practical sense.[208]

Lessons for the future

Capitalism has transformed itself, human society and the face of the planet since 1867. Yet its essentials persist, albeit in modified forms: private ownership of the means of production, distribution and exchange; generalised commodity production; the universal employment of labour power as a commodity; and the drive to maximise surplus value. So, too, does its primary contradiction remain: that between the relations of production — based on private ownership and the drive to maximise surplus value — and the forces of production, which are integrated and social.

All previous efforts to overthrow capitalism and begin the construction of a socialist system have taken place before that primary contradiction had matured. Capitalism's relations of production were not acting as an absolute barrier to any further development of society's forces of production, either in Russia in 1917, Eastern Europe in the 1940s, China in 1949, Cuba in 1959 nor Vietnam in 1971. Rather, revolutionary opportunities had arisen at particular points of imperialist crisis and dislocation that had weakened ruling class power sufficiently to allow its overthrow, other conditions permitting.

In all those cases and others, the construction of a new society took place in very specific circumstances nationally and internationally, which in turn played a major part in determining significant features of their embryonic socialist system. These conditions included relentless hostility in a world still dominated by major capitalist powers and economic, political and military imperialism.

Nonetheless, despite and because of their peculiarities, these first attempts at constructing socialism have furnished Marxist political economy with some rich experiences and lessons.

Firstly, society's material base must be constructed as an overriding priority if socialism is going to satisfy the most basic needs of its people and be able to defend itself. This may involve partial retreats and compromises with capitalist interests, together with the utilisation of mechanisms more characteristic of capitalist economies. Clearly, the dangers posed by such policies to socialist construction have to be recognised so that the necessary safeguards can be put in place.

This material basis is also the only basis for strengthening the working class numerically, economically, organisationally, politically and ideologically as the leading force in the revolutionary transition to communism. The Communist Party of Venezuela has been emphasising the centrality of this task in what is still an early stage in the revolutionary process in their country that is struggling to survive a coordinated onslaught from within and without. Likewise, the South African Communist Party puts the strengthening of the working class at the centre of every stage of its revolutionary programme.

Secondly, central economic planning and public ownership of key sectors of industry and commerce are essential mechanisms for controlling, directing and maximising society's productive forces. They played the predominant part in transforming the Soviet Union and several countries of Eastern Europe into modern, industrial and urban societies with substantial social and cultural provision for the mass of their peoples. The same is happening today in China. Moreover, the technological base is now being built that can eliminate some of the weaknesses and errors of previous attempts at central economic planning, such as the mismatches that arose between supply, demand and consumer preferences. As Wang and Li (2017) point out, enormous advances in data processing and 'artificial intelligence' could make it far easier to match the three in a system which seeks to combine central macro-economic planning, large-scale public enterprises and consumer-led demand.[209]

Thirdly, winning, maintaining and deploying state power is an essential pre-condition for abolishing the capitalist mode of production and constructing a socialist society. This can only be done at the level where that power continues to reside, where the capitalist class primarily exercises its rule — that of the national (or in Britain's case multinational) state. This is the case, even though numerous international institutions and relations exist within which ruling classes and states seek to cooperate in their common interests.

The European Union represents an advanced form of such international cooperation between capitalist state powers. In particular, it has been constructed in ways designed to outlaw, obstruct and undermine any attempts by elected national governments to introduce policies that would open the road to socialism, notably those to control the capital and labour markets, regulate and plan trade and investment, strategically extend public ownership across key sectors of the economy and utilise other mechanisms of state intervention in the capitalist 'free' (ie., monopoly dominated) market economy. Indeed, the EU's basic treaties explicitly commit the EU and its member states to sustain 'an open market economy with free competition'.[210] The functions and extensive powers of key EU institutions (the European Commission, the European Central Bank and the European Court of Justice) are defined accordingly. Although these institutions and their operations are placed beyond the control of democratically elected national governments, the facade of democracy at EU level is maintained by the existence of a largely powerless and remote European 'Parliament'.

Not surprisingly, therefore, monopoly capital and its politicians across Europe tend to be enthusiastically pro-EU, although contradictions and even divisions arise between the competing interests of big capitalists and between the different state-monopoly capitalisms. Certainly, most of the monopoly capitalist class in Britain — including the major City of London financial institutions — campaigned in favour of remaining in the EU in the 2016 referendum. Since their unexpected defeat, they have supported the drive to subvert if not overturn that decision, understanding — as the EU Commission has also pointed out — that Britain's continuing alignment with the EU Single Market and Customs Union represents a strong line of defence against the economic and social policies of a left-led Labour government.[211]

For most communist and workers' parties across Europe, therefore, repatriating powers from European Union institutions and mechanisms to democratically elected government at national, regional and local levels is a vital strategic goal in the struggle for socialism.

In its programme *Britain's Road to Socialism*, the Communist Party of Britain proposes the following perspective for a government and parliamentary majority of the left, backed by a mass movement:

> On the economic front, social ownership will have to be extended into the major enterprises in every significant sector of the economy including construction, engineering, armaments, land and property, shipping and chemicals, while consolidating the sectors already in public ownership. These measures would enable economic planning to develop in accordance with society's needs and objectives, combining local and sectoral consultation with centralised policy-making in strategic sectors, all under democratic control ...
> A substantial extension of democracy throughout the economy will have to take place, in cooperation with the trade unions, so that the knowledge, experience, interests and creativity of working people can be drawn fully into the processes of administration, decision-making and planning. Economic planning will also have to involve a wide range of other groups and forces in society besides government ministries and major enterprises, including local government, non-governmental organisations, consumer groups and community organisations.[212]

There are also some specific economic features of past and present socialist systems that offer valuable lessons for the future, for example how — and how not — to: develop and allocate the forces of production in a planned and balanced way; to introduce new technology while maintaining full employment; measure and stimulate economic performance and — not least — labour productivity; and distribute the product of surplus labour. Moreover, these contradictions will have to be resolved in an age when we understand much more about the vital necessity to pursue environmentally friendly and ecologically sustainable development.

Already, there are encouraging signs that countries which have taken a socialist road are formulating new and effective strategies to protect the eco-system. Alongside its short-term reliance on coal to fuel its fast-growing economy, China is investing massively in 'cutting-edge' research to pioneer clean energy technologies.[213] Cuba is one of the very few countries meeting two of the key minimum conditions set by the UN for sustainable development: a high level of human 'well-being for all' (measured by life expectancy, education, income) and a low ecological footprint (in terms of minimal productive space required per person).[214]

The full and permanent solutions to these and other problems will, of course, also have to be combined with those to political questions about the role of the working class, the people and their mass organisations in the exercise of state power on every front of communist construction, including in the workplace.

Echoing Marx's *Capital*, the Communist Party of Britain's programme envisages a future transition from the lower stage of communist society — socialism — to the higher stage:

> As cooperation, planning and the full application of science and technology begin to produce an abundance of the most important goods and services in society, so the principle in the higher stage of communism — full communism — becomes: 'From each according to their ability, to each according to their needs' ... the egotistical individualism of capitalism will be replaced by collective care and concern for every individual and for the full, all-round development of the human personality.[215]

Notes

1   Karl Marx & Frederick Engels, 'Economic Manuscripts of 1857-58', *Collected Works* (*MECW*) Vol 28 and Vol 29 pp 1-255.
2   *MECW* Vol 29 pp 257-417.
3   *MECW* Vol 29 p 263.
4   *MECW* Vols 30-34.
5   Nicholas Dimsdale & Anthony Hotson, eds., *British Financial Crises since 1825* (Oxford, 2014) pp 50-51.
6   See *MECW* Vol 15 pp 379-84, 400-18, 459-63.
7   See, for example, 'British Commerce and Finance', *New York Daily Tribune*, 4 October 1858, *MECW* Vol 16 pp 33-36.
8   *MECW* Vol 35 p 45.
9   *MECW* Vol 32 p 174.
10 Vitor Leoni & Bruce Philip, 'Surplus Value and Concentration in the UK Economy, 1987-2009' at https://www4.ntu.ac.uk/nbs/document_uploads/102531.pdf.
11 Michael Roberts, 'Debating the Rate of Profit' at https://thenextrecession.wordpress.com/2016/11/10/debating-the-rate-of-profit/.
12 *MECW* Vol 28 p 336.
13 *MECW* Vol 35 p 405.
14 *MECW* Vol 35 p 464.
15 Table XVIII, Census of England and Wales for the Year 1861 (1863); industrial workers plus general labourers, minus workers in construction, mines and quarries.
16 Calculated from Tables XX and XIX, Census of England and Wales for the Year 1861 (1863).
17 *MECW* Vol 35 p 398.
18 *MECW* Vol 35 p 406.
19 *MECW* Vol 35 p 399.
20 *MECW* Vol 35 p 397.
21 *MECW* Vol 35 pp 261-62.
22 *MECW* 35 pp 264-65.
23 *MECW* Vol 35 p 293.
24 *MECW* Vol 35 pp 299-300.
25 *MECW* Vol 35 p 401; see also pp 298, 402.
26 *MECW* Vol 35 p 450.
27 Table XVIII, Census of England and Wales for the Year 1861 (1863).
28 *MECW* Vol 35 pp 465-66.
29 *MECW* Vol 35 p 472.
30 *MECW* Vol 35 p 473.
31 *MECW* Vol 35 pp 492-93.
32 *MECW* Vol 21 pp 382-83.
33 See notes 383 and 384, *MECW* Vol 46 pp 637-38.
34 F Engels to Gertrud Guillaume-Schack, circa 5 July 1885, *MECW* Vol 47 pp 311-12.
35 International Labour Organisation, *World Employment Social Outlook: Trends for Women 2017* (2017).
36 Sheila Wild, http://www.equalpayportal.co.uk/statistics/.
37 European Trade Union Institute at http://www.worker-participation.eu/National-Industrial-Relations/Across-Europe/Trade-Unions2#_ftn10; Eurofound at https://www.eurofound.europa.eu/observatories/eurwork/comparative-information/trade-union-membership-2003-2008; Japan International Labour Foundation, '206 Survey on Trade Unions' at http://www.jilaf.or.jp/eng/mbn/2017/227.html; for the USA, see Cherrie

Bucknor, 'Union Membership Byte 2017' at http://cepr.net/images/stories/reports/union-byte-2017-01.pdf?v=2. Density statistics are notoriously inconsistent, calculated on the basis of different variables (including/excluding retired union members as a percentage of employees/total labour force including employers, self-employed and unemployed).

38   Department for Business, Energy & Industrial Strategy, https://www.gov.uk/government/statistics/trade-union-statistics-2017.

39   *MECW* Vol 35 p 430-35.

40   *MECW* Vol 29 p 209.

41   ILO, *Workplace Stress: A Collective Challenge* (2016); Trades Union Congress, *Focus on health and safety* (2016).

42   *MECW* Vol 3 p 274.

43   *MECW* Vol 35 p 455.

44   *MECW* Vol 28 p 338.

45   Organisation for Economic Co-operation and Development, https://stats.oecd.org/index.aspx; for detailed figures for the 1950-98 period, see Angus Maddison, *The World Economy: A Millennial Perspective* (OECD, 2001).

46   *MECW* Vol 35 p 621.

47   *MECW* Vol 35 p 627.

48   See, for example, *MECW* Vol 35 pp 397-508.

49   *MECW* Vol 26 p 626.

50   *MECW* Vol 35 p 739.

51   *MECW* Vol 35 p 747; see also the classic work by Eric Williams, *Capitalism and Slavery* (1944).

52   *MECW* Vol 35 p 748.

53   *MECW* Vol 35 p 750.

54   VI Lenin, *Imperialism: the Highest Stage of Capitalism* (1916), *Collected Works* Vol 22 pp 266-67.

55   *MECW* Vol 37 p 255.

56   International Monetary Fund, *World Economic Outlook* (October 2018) data mapper at https://www.imf.org/external/datamapper/NGDPD@WEO/OEMDC/ADVEC/WEOWORLD/ROU

57   Forbes, 'The World's Biggest Public Companies' at https://www.forbes.com/global2000/list/;

58   Torsten Bell & Dan Tomlinson, Is everybody concentrating? Recent trends in product and labour market concentration in the UK (Resolution Foundation, July 2018) at https://www.resolutionfoundation.org/app/uploads/2018/07/Is-everybody-concentrating_Recent-trends-in-product-and-labour-market-concentration-in-the-UK.pdf.

59. BEIS analysis of key sectors (by SIC 2007) at https://assets.publishing.service.gov.uk/government/uploads/system/uploads/attachment_data/file/598726/Sector_analysis_0317.xls.]

60   See, for example, Jason Furman, 'Beyond Antitrust: The Role of Competition Policy in Promoting Inclusive Growth' (2016) at https://obamawhitehouse.archives.gov/sites/default/files/page/files/20160916_searle_conference_competition_furman_cea.pdf.

61   Council of Economic Advisers Issue Brief, 'Benefits of competition and indicators of market power', April 2016.

62   For sources and discussion, see Bell & Tomlinson (2018) and OECD 'Market Concentration — Note by Jason Furman', 7 June 2018. Like many other economists, these authors use the term 'concentration' to cover both concentration and centralisation.

63   ONS, Concentration ratios for businesses by industry in 2004 (2006) p 139.

64   F Engels, 'Introduction to Sigismund Borkheim's Pamphlet, etc.', *MECW* Vol 26 p 451.

65   *MECW* Vol 35 p 750.

66   François Bourguignon & Christian Morrisson, 'Inequality among World Citizens: 1820-

1992', *The American Economic Review*, Vol 92, No 4 (Sep. 2002).
67 Max Roser & Esteban Ortiz-Ospina, 'Global Health', at https://ourworldindata.org/health-meta.
68 Max Roser & Esteban Ortiz-Ospina, 'Income Inequality', https://ourworldindata.org/income-inequality/.
69 World Top Incomes Database at https://old.datahub.io/dataset/world-top-incomes-database.
70 Calculated from ONS, 'The Effects of Taxes and Benefits on Household Income' (20 June 2018) Table 2a available at https://www.ons.gov.uk/peoplepopulationandcommunity/personalandhouseholdfinances/inc omeandwealth/datasets/theeffectsoftaxesandbenefitsonhouseholdincomefinancialyearendin g2014.
71 Thomas Piketty, *Capital in the Twenty-first Century* (2014); Fig. 10.3 online at http://piketty.pse.ens.fr/files/capital21c/en/pdf/F10.3.pdf.
72 Calculated from ONS, *Wealth in Great Britain Wave 5: 2014 to 2016* (2018) at https://www.ons.gov.uk/releases/wealthingreatbritainwave52014to2016.
73 Calculated from tables in note 69 above.
74 Richard Murphy, *The Tax Gap: Tax evasion in 2014 and what can be done about it* (2014).
75 Details of the investigations by the International Consortium of Investigative Journalists can be found at https://www.icij.org/investigations/.
76 Piketty (2014) Figs 6.1 and 6.2 online at http://piketty.pse.ens.fr/files/capital21c/en/pdf/F6.1.pdf (Britain) and http://piketty.pse.ens.fr/files/capital21c/en/pdf/F6.2.pdf (France).
77 Emmanuel Saez and Gabriel Zucman, 'Wealth Inequality in the United States since 1913' (October 2014) at http://gabriel-zucman.eu/files/SaezZucman2014Slides.pdf.
78 'Value, Price and Profit', *MECW* Vol 20 pp 101-49.
79 International Labour Organisation, http://www.ilo.org/global/statistics-and-databases/lang--en/index.htm.
80 World Bank, *East Asia & Pacific Update: 10 years after the crisis* (April 2007).
81 UN Food and Agriculture Organisation, *The State of Food Insecurity in the World* (2015).
82 82 François Bourguignon & Christian Morrisson (Sep. 2002); World Bank estimates at http://blogs.worldbank.org/developmenttalk/april-2018-global-poverty-update-world-bank; http://www.worldbank.org/en/news/press-release/2018/09/19/decline-of-global-extreme-poverty-continues-but-has-slowed-world-bank; and http://www.worldbank.org/en/news/press-release/2018/10/17/nearly-half-the-world-lives-on-less-than-550-a-day.
83 Utsa Patnaik, 'Capitalism and the Production of Poverty', *Social Scientist* (New Delhi), Vol 40, No. 1/2 (January-February 2012); reprinted in *Communist Review* no 75 (Spring 2015).
84 *MECW* vol 35 p 647.
85 Karl Marx to Johann Philipp Becker, 17 April 1867, *MECW* Vol.42 p.358.
86 More information can be found at http://www.post-crasheconomics.com/economics-education-and-unlearning/ and http://www.bbc.co.uk/news/business-35462879.
87 Email from JH to the author, 26 March 2015.
88 *MECW* Vol 34 p 131.
89 *MECW* Vol 35 p 510.
90 *MECW* Vol 35 p 510.
91 *MECW* Vol 34 p 144.
92 Ian Gough, 'Marx's Theory of Productive and Unproductive Labour', *New Left Review* no. 76, November/December 1972; online at http://personal.lse.ac.uk/goughi/Gough%20NLR%2076.pdf.
93 See, for example, *MECW* Vol 36 pp 62, 153-54.
94 *MECW* Vol 37 p 292.

95 *MECW* Vol 37 pp 278-79.
96 In the second article of the series on which this book is based, I expressed the view that: 'For Marx, then, the outlay on such unproductive labour comprises part of the variable capital v and is not reflected in the surplus value s created within the capitalist economy as a whole'; see Robert Griffiths, 'Marx's *Capital* and capitalism today, Part 2', *Communist Review*, No 86, Winter 2017/2018. Further re-reading of texts by Marx and Marxist political economists such as Gough (1972) and David Harvey, *Companion to Marx's Capital: Volume II* (2013 edn) has led me to withdraw this assessment. Indeed, I am not convinced by Harvey's conclusion that the problems raised by the productive/non-productive labour dichotomy are 'insoluble' (p92)!
97 *MECW* Vol 37 p 299.
98 *MECW* Vol 37 p 235.
99 *MECW* Vol 35 p 255.
100 *MECW* Vol 37 pp 235-37.
101 Ljubica Nedelkoska and Glenda Quintini, 'Automation, skills use and training', 14 March 2018; online at: https://www.oecd-ilibrary.org/employment/automation-skills-use-and-training_2e2f4eea-en.
102 *MECW* Vol 35 pp 614-16.
103 *MECW* Vol 37 p 238.
104 *MECW* Vol 37 p 242.
105 Michael Roberts, 'UK rate of profit and British economic history' (2015a) at https://thenextrecession.files.wordpress.com/2015/09/uk-rate-of-profit-august-2015.pdf.
106 Esteban E Maito, The historical transience of capital: the downward trend in the rate of profit since XIX century (2014) https://mpra.ub.uni-muenchen.de/55894/1/.
107 Minqi Li, Feng Xiao & Andong Zhu, 'Long Waves, Institutional Changes, and Historical Trends: A study of the Long-Term Movement of the Profit Rate in the Capitalist World-Economy' (2007) at http://jwsr.pitt.edu/ojs/index.php/jwsr/article/view/360.
108 Michael Roberts, 'Revisiting a world rate of profit' (2015b) at https://thenextrecession.files.wordpress.com/2015/12/revisiting-a-world-rate-of-profit-june-2015.pdf.
109 Peter Jones, 'The Falling Rate of Profit Explains Falling US Growth' (2013) at https://thenextrecession.files.wordpress.com/2013/12/jones-the-falling-rate-of-profit-explains-falling-us-growth-v2.pdf.
110 Michael Roberts, 'Measuring the rate of profit; profit cycles and the next recession' (2011) at https://thenextrecession.files.wordpress.com/2011/07/the-profit-cycle-and-economic-recession.pdf.
111 Themistoklis Kalogerakos, 'Financialization, the Great Recession, and the rate of profit: profitability trends in the US corporate business sector, 1946-2011' (2013) at https://thenextrecession.files.wordpress.com/2013/12/ekhr6_themistoklis_kalogerakos.pdf.
112 For a Marxist critique of Piketty, see Prabhat Patnaik, 'Capital, Inequality and Globalization: Thomas Piketty's *Capital in the Twenty-first Century*', *The Marxist* (New Delhi) Vol 30 no 2 (April-June 2014), online at http://cpim.org/sites/default/files/marxist/201402-marxist-prabhat.pdf; reprinted in *Communist Review* (Britain) No 74 (Winter 2014/15).
113 See, for instance, Alan Peacock, 'Economics of a Net Wealth Tax for Britain', *British Tax Review*, November/December 1963, and CT Sandford, JRM Willis & DJ Ironside, *An Annual Wealth Tax* (1975). The 1974 Labour government established a Royal Commission on the Distribution of Income and Wealth, but introduced a corporation tax on company profits and a capital gains tax on asset sales in place of the promised annual wealth tax. See Howard Glennerster, 'Why was a wealth tax for the UK abandoned?: lessons for the policy process and tackling wealth inequality' at http://eprints.lse.ac.uk/42582/1/Why_was_a_wealth_tax_for_the_UK_abandoned_%28lse

ro%29.pdf

114 Mervyn King review, *The Telegraph*, 10 May 2014, at
https://www.telegraph.co.uk/culture/books/bookreviews/10816161/Capital-in-the-Twenty-First-Century-by-Thomas-Piketty-review.html; Chris Giles, 'Data problems with
http://blogs.ft.com/money-supply/2014/05/23/data-problems-with-capital-in-the-21st-century/ and 'Piketty findings undercut by errors'; Chris Giles and Ferdinando Giugliano, 'Thomas Piketty's exhaustive inequality data turn out to be flawed'; *Financial Times*, 23 May 2014; Thomas Piketty, 'Technical appendix of the book *Capital in the Twenty-first Century*. Appendix to chapter 10. Inequality of Capital Ownership. Addendum: Response to FT, 28 May 2014, at
http://piketty.pse.ens.fr/files/capital21c/en/Piketty2014TechnicalAppendixResponsetoFT.pdf.

115 Ben Fine, *Marx's Capital* (2016) p 62, in the series of Macmillan Studies in Economics.

116 See, for instance, Andrew Kliman, *Reclaiming Marx's 'Capital': A Refutation of the Myth of Inconsistency* (2007).

117 For a concise discussion of these and other controversies up to the time of its publication, see Ben Fine & Laurence Harris, 'Controversial Issues in Marxist Economic Theory', *The Socialist Register*, 1976.

118 *MECW* Vol.37 p.483.

119 Michael Kidron, 'A Permanent Arms Economy', *International Socialism* no. 28 (Spring 1967).

120 Joan Robinson, *Essays in the Theory of Economic Growth* (1962) p.92.

121 Michael Kidron, 'Two Insights Don't Make a Theory', *International Socialism* no.100, July 1977.

122 Michael Roberts, 'UK rate of profit and British economic history' (2015) at
https://thenextrecession.files.wordpress.com/2015/09/uk-rate-of-profit-august-2015.pdf.

123 *MECW* Vol 37 p 400.

124 *MECW* Vol 31 pp 470-71.

125 *MECW* Vol 31 p 470.

126 *MECW* Vol 37 p 240.

127 *MECW* Vol 37 p 509.

128 *MECW* Vol 32 p 464.

129 Luiz Carlos Bresser-Pereira, 'The Global Financial Crisis and a New Capitalism?' (2010) p 12 at http://www.levyinstitute.org/pubs/wp_592.pdf.

130 Veronika Stolbova, Stefano Battiston, Mauro Napoletano & Andrea Roventini, *Financialization of Europe: a comparative perspective* (2017) at http://www.isigrowth.eu/wp-content/uploads/2017/07/working_paper_2017_22.pdf.

131 *MECW* Vol 37 p 489. For an interesting discussion of this and related points, see Michael Hudson, 'From Marx to Goldman Sachs: The Fictions of Fictitious Capital, and the Financialization of Industry', *Critique*, Vol.3 Issue 38, 2010.

132 Michael Roberts, 'Revisiting a world rate of profit' (2015) at
https://thenextrecession.files.wordpress.com/2015/12/revisiting-a-world-rate-of-profit-june-2015.pdf; and 'Cycles in capitalism' (2013) at
https://thenextrecession.files.wordpress.com/2013/07/cycles-in-capitalism.pdf; Esteban E Maito (2014).

133 Alan Freeman, 'The Profit Rate in the Presence of Financial Markets: a Necessary Correction' (2012) at https://mpra.ub.uni-muenchen.de/52625/1/MPRA_paper_52625.pdf.

134 Quarterly Growth Rates of real GDP, change over previous quarter, at
stats.oecd.org/index.aspx.

135 World Bank Group, *World Development Report: The Changing Nature of Work* (2018) available at http://documents.worldbank.org/curated/en/816281518818814423/pdf/2019-WDR-Report.pdf.

136 See also Larry Elliott, 'World Bank recommends fewer regulations protecting workers', *The Guardian*, 20 April 2018.

137 Institute for Mergers, Acquisitions and Alliances, https://imaa-institute.org/mergers-and-acquisitions-statistics/.

138 F Engels, *Dialectics of Nature*, MECW Vol 25.

139 See John Bellamy Foster, 'Late Soviet Ecology and the Planetary Crisis', *Monthly Review* Vol 67 No 2 (June 2015).

140 *MECW* Vol 35 p 187.

141 *MECW* Vol 35 p 513.

142 *MECW* Vol 35 p 53.

143 *MECW* Vol 35 pp 507, 669.

144 *MECW* Vol 37 p 768.

145 *MECW* Vol 35 p 508.

146 *MECW* Vol 37 pp 102-5.

147 *MECW* Vol 37 p 92.

148 *MECW* Vol 37 pp 103.

149. *MECW* Vol 35 pp 506; see John Bellamy Foster, *Marx's Ecology: Materialism and Nature* (2000) and John Bellamy Foster, Brett Clark & Richard York, *The Ecological Rift: Capitalism's War on the Earth* (2010). The authors prefer a more modern translation whereby capitalist production 'disturbs the metabolic interaction between man and the earth'.

150 *MECW* Vol 35 pp 508.

151 *MECW* Vol 37 pp 799-800. Some writers prefer a more modern translation whereby large landed property 'produces conditions that provoke an irreparable rift in the interdependent process of social metabolism, a metabolism prescribed by the natural laws of life itself'. Much of the quotation from Marx is itself derived from Justus Liebig, *Die Chemie in ihrer Anwendung auf Agricultur und Physiologie* (1862).

152 *MECW* Vol 35 pp 506-7.

153 *MECW* Vol 37 p 611.

154 IPCC, Global Warming of 1.5°C (October 2018) available at http://www.ipcc.ch/report/sr15/.

155 *MECW* Vol 35 p 89.

156 *MECW* Vol 35 p 104.

157 *MECW* Vol 24 pp 86-87.

158 *MECW* Vol 35 p 530.

159 *MECW* Vol 35 p 396.

160 *MECW* Vol 29 p 97.

161 *MECW* Vol 29 pp 209-10.

162 *MECW* Vol 36 p 314.

163 *MECW* Vol 36 pp 314-15.

164 *MECW* Vol 35 p 468.

165 *MECW* Vol 6 p 490.

166 *MECW* Vol 37 p 186.

167 *MECW* Vol 37 p 806.

168 *MECW* Vol 37 p 807.

169 *MECW* Vol 35 p 484-85.

170 *MECW* Vol 35 p 486.

171 *MECW* Vol 37 p 799.

172 *MECW* Vol 37 p 807.

173 *MECW* Vol 37 p 763.

174 See, for example, John Bellamy Foster (note 149); Douglas Weiner, *Models of Nature: Ecology, Conservation and Cultural Revolution in Soviet Russia* (1988) and *A Little Corner*

of Freedom: Russian Nature Protection from Stalin to Gorbachev (1999); and William M. Mandel, 'The Soviet Ecology Movement', *Science & Society*, Vol 36 No 4 (Winter, 1972).]

175 *MECW* Vol 37 p 242.

176 JV Stalin, *Economic problems of the USSR* (1952) in *Collected Works*, Vol 16.

177 J Wilczynski, *Profit, Risk and Incentives under Socialist Economic Planning* (1973), especially Ch 4, 'Prices and profits', pp 81, 90, 95, 106.

178 Calculated from Maddison (2001), pp 187, 272, 273, 275, 298, 329. For an interesting discussion of differing estimates of Soviet economic growth, see Mark Harrison, 'Soviet Economic Growth Since 1928: The Alternative Statistics of G.I. Khanin', *Europe-Asia Studies*, Vol 45, No 1, 1993.

179 United Nations, *Yearbook of Industrial Statistics*, various years.

180 For a useful overview and analysis of this debate, see Marc Trachtenberg, 'Assessing Soviet Economic Performance during the Cold War: A Failure of Intelligence?', *Texas National Security Review* Vol 1 Issue 2 (February 2018) available at https://repositories.lib.utexas.edu/handle/2152/63942; Mark Harrison's assessment of GI Khanin's dissident calculations — and of official Soviet and US statistics — is very informative, although he is more sympathetic to Khanin than some of his own conclusions in relation to the pre-war plans and the late 1960s would seem to warrant. See Harrison, 'Soviet Economic Growth Since 1928: The Alternative Statistics of GI Khanin', *Europe-Asia Studies* Vol 45 No 1 (1993).

181 For a comprehensive and readily available survey of the Soviet economy and related debates and assessments — without accepting all of his conclusions — see Philip Hanson, *The Rise and Fall of the Soviet Economy: An Economic History of the USSR from 1945* (2003) at http://www.ie.ufrj.br/intranet/ie/userintranet/hpp/arquivos/021020175828_PhilipHansonTheRiseandFalloftheTheSovietEconomy_AnEconomicHistoryoftheUSSRfrom1945Longman _PearsonEducationLimited20031.pdf.

182 Available at www.marxists.org/archive/cliff/works/1955/statecap/index.htm.

183 VI Lenin, *The Impending Catastrophe and How to Combat It* (1917), *Collected Works*, Vol 25 p 363.

184 *MECW* Vol 35 pp 164, 165.

185 *China Statistical Yearbook 2017*, Table 13.1, figures for 2016.

186 'The 13th Five-Year Plan: For Economic and Social Development of the People's Republic of China' (2016-2020) at http://en.ndrc.gov.cn/newsrelease/201612/P020161207645765233498.pdf

187 Scott Cendrowski, 'China's Global 500 companies are bigger than ever—and mostly state-owned', http://fortune.com/2015/07/22/china-global-500-government-owned/.

188 'Constitution of the Communist Party of China' (2017) at http://www.china.org.cn/20171105-001.pdf.

189 US Mission to the WTO, 'China's Trade-Disruptive Economic Model', 11 July 2018, available at: https://docs.wto.org/dol2fe/Pages/SS/directdoc.aspx?filename=q:/WT/GC/W745.pdf.

190 For beginners, a short but comprehensive account of China's development and perspectives can be found in Bernard Chavance, 'Ownership Transformation and System Change in China' at http://journals.openedition.org/regulation/12298.

191 *MECW* Vol 35 p 505.

192 *MECW* Vol 35 p 304.

193 *MECW* Vol 37 pp 385-86.

194 See https://www.thenews.coop/96859/sector/retail/mondragon-created-1000-new-jobs-2014/.

195 Sharryn Kasmir, *The Myth of Mondragon: Cooperatives, Politics, and Working-Class Life in a Basque Town* (1996).

196 ILO, 'Rebuilding links: Trade unions and cooperatives get together again', 22 May 2014, http://www.ilo.org/global/about-the-ilo/newsroom/news/WCMS_243813/lang--en/index.htm.

197 *MECW* Vol 37 p 438.

198 *MECW* Vol 24 pp 296-97.

199 VI Lenin, On Co-operation (1923), *Collected Works*, Vol 33 p 468.

200 Frederick A Leedy, 'Producers' Cooperatives in the Soviet Union', *Monthly Labor Review*, Vol 80 no 9 (September 1957).

201 *Statistical Yearbooks of the Czechoslovak Republic.*

202 Ferenc Fekete, *Economics of Cooperative Farming: Objectives and Optima in Hungary* (2013).

203 Mieke Meurs, *Many Shades of Red: State Policy and Collective Agriculture* (1999) p 100.

204 http://www.housinginternational.coop/co-ops/poland.

205 Bengt Turner, Jozsef Hegedus & Ivan Tosics eds, *The Reform of Housing in Eastern Europe and the Soviet Union* (1992).

206 Martin McCauley, *The German Democratic Republic since 1945* (2016).

207 All China Federation of Supply and Marketing Co-operatives, https://ica.coop/en/directory/member/100.

208 See Russell Smith, 'Co-operative Ownership and Control at Tower Colliery: the Creation of a Human Firm?', *Journal of Co-operative Studies* Vol 48 No 2 (No 144) Autumn 2015, online at https://ukscs.coop/sites/default/files/S02-MaddocksHicks-144.pdf.

209 Binbin Wang & Xiaoyan Li, 'Big Data, Platform Economy and Market Competition: A Preliminary Construction of Plan-Orienated Market Economy System in the Information Era', *World Review of Political Economy*, Vol 8 No 2 (Beijing, Summer 2017); for a summary, see also 'The Big Data revolution can revive the planned economy', *Financial Times*, 4 September 2017.

210 Treaty on the Functioning of the European Union, Articles 119,120 and 127; see also Treaty on European Union, Article 3.

211 See, for example, 'Fear of Jeremy Corbyn-led government prompts tough EU line on Brexit/ Brussels vows to protect single market from Labour's left⊠wing policies', *The Times*, 7 May 2018; 'UK Brexit team seeks to exploit EU concern over Corbyn state aid plans/ Exclusive: Chequers plan ties future governments to EU rules on subsidies, negotiators say', *The Guardian*, 2 August 2018; 'Corbyn ditches consensus to reject EU trade deals', *Financial Times*, 4 August 2018.

212 Communist Party of Britain, *Britain's Road to Socialism* (2011) p 34.

213 Mark Peplow, 'China powers up', *Chemistry World*, 23 February 2018; online at https://www.chemistryworld.com/feature/renewable-energy-in-china/3008533.article.

214 Global Footprint Network, 'Only eight countries meet two key conditions for sustainable development as United Nations adopts Sustainable Development Goals', 23 September 2015; online at https://www.footprintnetwork.org/2015/09/23/eight-countries-meet-two-key-conditions-sustainable-development-united-nations-adopts-sustainable-development-goals/

215 *Britain's Road to Socialism* (2011) p 35.

Index

A

A Contribution to the Critique of Political Economy (ACCPE) 1
accountancy, socialist 69
Afghanistan 65
Africa 11, 17, 18, 26, 31, 79
agriculture 9, 12, 16, 17, 18, 31, 54-57, 62, 63, 65, 70; agribusiness 56, 76; agrochemicals 24;
  cooperative 70, 75, 76, 77; under socialism 65, 70, 71, 75, 76, 77; women in 9; workers in 9, 31, 56;
  see peasantry
Albania 75
alienation ('estrangement') 13, 14, 59
All-China Federation of Trade Unions 30
American Civil War 1, 7
anarchism 66, 69
anarchy, capitalist 32, 37, 58, 59
anti-communism 29, 43, 65, 66
anti-Sovietism 43, 65, 66
Argentina 44
armaments 46, 47, 66, 70, 80
'artificial intelligence' 39, 79
artisan or handicraft labour 6, 13, 19, 70, 71, 75, 76, 77
'associated producers' 60, 61, 72
austerity 50, 52
Australia 1, 5, 16, 18, 22, 23
Austria 12
automation 13, 14, 39, 85

B

banks or banking 1, 8, 19, 20, 23, 24, 28, 35, 48, 49, 50, 52, 72, 77, 78; bailouts 47, 50, 52
Basque Country 73
Bath, University of 33
Belgium 12, 21, 30
Bettelheim, Charles 69
Beveridge, William 16
BNP Paribas 21, 50
boom, economic 1, 2, 14, 16, 40
Bourguignon, François 26, 83, 84
Brazil 20, 26, 33, 73
'breadwinner's wage' 11
Britain's Road to Socialism 80, 81
Bucharest Agreement 68
Bukharin, Nikolai 62
Bulgaria 12, 30, 68, 76
Burnham, James 67

C

Canada 18, 20, 74
capital, accumulation of 5, 14, 16, 32, 38, 39, 40, 44, 49, 50, 60, 66, 68; centralisation of 16, 19, 23-25,
  83; circulating 36, 42, 69; commercial 35, 36, 47, 48, 61; composition of 37, 38, 41, 43, 51;
  concentration of 16, 19, 24, 25; constant 4, 5, 38, 42, 52; 'fictitious' 43, 47-53; finance 19, 24, 31, 50;
  fixed 42, 52; global tax on 43, 44; organic composition of 37, 38, 39, 41, 42, 43, 46, 47, 51; over-
  accumulation of 14, 49, 52; primitive accumulation of 17-19, 31; technical composition of 38; turnover
  of 16; values 40, 51, 52; variable 4, 34, 38, 42, 85; see monopolisation

capitalist class 5-9, 11, 14, 16, 19, 25, 26, 34, 37, 38, 39, 40, 45, 48, 53, 58, 60, 61, 66, 67, 69, 73, 79, 80; industrial section of 7, 8, 17-19, 35, 36, 48, 49, 61

capitalist mode of production 1, 2, 4, 6, 9, 10, 15-19, 25, 29, 31, 32, 34, 36, 40-42, 47, 49, 51, 52, 54-57, 59, 60, 62, 63, 65, 69, 72, 73, 74, 78, 85

carbon capture or emissions 57

Caribbean 12

Castro, Raoul 77

casual work 17

Chicago, University School of 46, 47

child labour 6-10, 12, 13, 18, 32, 59, 61

child mortality rates 9, 26

Children's Employment Commission 8, 10

Chile 30, 47

China 17, 18, 20, 26, 30, 31, 33, 51, 57, 70-73, 77-79, 81

circulation, economic sphere of 4, 5, 35, 45, 47

City of London 24, 50, 80

class struggle 6, 13, 30, 69, 75; economic 5, 6, 13, 25, 28-30, 42, 43; ideological 12, 33, 47, 64, 65, 74, 79; revolutionary (political) 25, 30, 36, 75, 78, 79, 81

clerical work 12, 29, 35

Cliff, Tony 46, 66-69

climate change 56

climatology 62

coal industry or miners 7, 8, 11, 24, 77, 78, 81

collective bargaining 5, 12, 13, 42, 53

collective or social labour 18, 19, 25, 34, 35, 60, 61, 72

colonialism 17, 18, 19, 25, 26, 31

COMECON 65, 68, 69

commercial capital or profit 35, 36, 47, 48, 61

commercial workers 29, 35, 36, 47, 48

commodities 1-6, 14, 17, 18, 24, 34, 35-37, 38, 40, 47, 48, 49, 51, 55, 58, 59, 60, 62, 63, 68, 69, 78; over-production of 2, 14, 40, 49, 51, 59

communist mode of production 2, 57, 58-61, 62, 65, 67, 72, 75, 79, 81; higher stage of 67, 81; lower stage of 62, 67, 81; see socialism

communist parties of Britain 80, 81; Bulgaria 76; China 18, 70-72; France 29; South Africa 79; Soviet Union 30, 62, 63, 65, 66; Venezuela 79; Yugoslavia 77

competition, capitalist 14, 16, 19, 38, 55, 58, 65, 74, 79

computerisation 14, 39

Confederation of Shipbuilding and Engineering Unions 5

Conservative Party 16, 45, 47

construction industry 18, 20, 57, 76, 80

consumption, capitalist 3, 5, 16, 40, 43, 45, 55, 62, 63, 67

cooperation, labour process 18, 19, 34, 35, 60, 61, 72, 81

cooperatism or cooperatives 58, 61, 65, 70, 72-78

Corbyn, Jeremy 89

Corn Laws 54

Corporation Tax 85

Council for Mutual Economic Assistance (COMECON) 65, 68, 69

credit 1, 2, 15-18, 24, 48, 49, 51, 71, 74-77; unions 77

Crimean War 2

crises, capitalist 1, 2, 14, 15, 36, 40, 45-46, 59; of disproportion 36; financial 2, 47-53; of over-production 2, 14, 15, 40, 51, 52, 59

Critique of the Gotha Programme 58

Cuba 65, 77, 78, 81

cycles, business or capitalist 2, 14, 15, 40, 41-43, 45, 47, 51, 52

Cyprus 12, 30

Czechoslovakia 30, 75, 76, 77

D

debt 15, 28, 49, 50, 52
demand, economic 3, 15, 33, 36-38, 45, 46, 60, 62-64, 79
Denmark 5
Department I (producer goods) 37-40, 59, 63
Department II (consumer goods) 37, 40
depreciation 4, 51
depression, capitalist 15, 29, 42, 45, 52, 65
deregulation 33, 46, 50
deskilling 6
developed countries 6, 12, 13, 15, 19, 25, 26, 30, 44, 56, 59, 75, 77
developing or Third World countries 11, 12, 18, 26, 31, 42, 47, 51, 65, 68
development, economic 1, 2, 13, 15, 18, 19, 25, 26, 32, 49, 53, 56, 57, 61, 70, 72, 74, 78, 80, 81
dividends 27, 28, 48, 52
domestic servants or service 9, 12, 45

E

Eastern Europe, socialism in 30, 33, 49, 63-65, 75, 78, 79
ecology 54, 62, 71, 80, 81
Economic and Philosophical Manuscripts (1844) 14
economic base, society's 32, 65, 67, 70, 74, 78, 79
Economic Manuscripts (1863-65) 1; (1857-58) 1, 2, 13, 14, 32, 44, 59; (1861-63) 1, 4, 34, 35
education 6, 12, 31, 33, 34, 36, 45, 53, 61, 66, 72, 76, 81
employment rights 11, 12, 46
Engels, Frederick 1, 11, 25, 33, 37, 48, 49, 54, 59, 62, 67, 75
engineering 5, 15, 35, 59, 80
Engineering Employers Federation 5
environmental matters 26, 31, 32, 54, 62, 71, 80
equal pay see 11-13
'estrangement' or alienation 13, 14, 59
European Central Bank 50, 79
European Commission 50, 79
European Union (EU) 5, 44, 49, 50, 53, 79, 80, 89
Euzkadi (Basque Country) 73
exchange-value 2-4, 6, 34, 35, 37, 38, 48, 56, 60, 62, 63, 68, 69
expanded reproduction 4, 5, 14, 16, 38, 42, 44, 46, 49, 51
Exploitation, Theory of Labour 1, 2, 5, 42, 43
exploitation of labour, capitalist 1, 2, 4, 5, 7, 8, 9-12, 16, 19, 25, 26, 30, 36, 39-42, 47, 52, 53, 67; of child labour 6-10, 12, 13, 18, 32, 59; of women 6-13, 59; super-exploitation 13, 19, 53;
exploitation or surplus value, rate of 4, 7, 19, 40-42, 47, 68
export of capital 19, 47
expropriation, capitalist 16, 17, 18, 19, 77
expropriation, socialist 25, 67, 70, 77
extended reproduction see expanded reproduction

F

factory system 7-11, 15, 35, 61, 72-74; legislative reforms 8-10, 11, 13; women workers in 7-10
family, capitalism and 7, 10, 11, 18
fascism or Nazism 66, 67, 68
feudalism 1, 17, 19
'fictitious' capital 43, 47-53, 86
Financial Times 43, 44, 86, 89
finance capital 19, 24, 31, 50
financial crises (1847) 48; (1857-58) 1, 2; Wall Street (1929) 29, 41; 'Great Crash' (2007-08) 33, 50-53
financialisation 47, 50, 52, 53
financial markets 24, 49-52, 53

First World War 25, 26, 27, 28, 41, 67
Five Year Plans, China 70, 71; Soviet Union 62, 75
food or nutrition 3, 8, 9, 30-32, 55, 59, 60, 75, 77
forces of production 1, 5, 13, 25, 32, 36, 45, 58, 60, 61, 69, 72, 74, 78, 79
forests or forestry 12, 54, 56, 62
France 1, 5, 15, 17-20, 28, 29, 33, 44, 46, 63, 64, 74

G

gender, inequality 7-12; pay gap 12
Germany 1, 5, 12, 15, 17, 19, 20, 30, 33, 42, 43, 46, 49, 57, 67, 68; German Democratic Republic 65, 76,77; West Germany 46, 63, 64
global inequality 26, 30, 31; population 30; poverty 30, 31; tax on capital 43, 44
global warming 31, 56, 57
globalisation 14, 19, 31, 44, 49, 70, 71
Gorbachev, Mikhail 65
Gough, Ian 35
Great Depression (1929-32) 29, 42, 45
Great War (1914-1918) 25, 26, 27, 28, 41, 67
Grenada 5
Guevara, Che 62

H

Hallas, Duncan 46
handicraft or artisan labour 6, 13, 70, 71, 77
Harvey, David 85
health or healthcare 6, 9, 11, 12, 26, 60, 66, 72
Highland Clearances 17
historical materialism 1
homeworkers 9
household, debt 52; income 27, 28; production 71; wealth 28
housework 7, 9, 10, 13, 45
housing 32, 66, 76
Hungary 12, 30, 65, 76

I

immigration 16, 18; see migrant workers
immiseration or pauperisation 25, 26, 29, 31
imperialism 13, 19, 25, 26, 31, 41, 49, 65-68, 71, 78
Imperialism: the Highest Stage of Imperialism 19, 83
income and wealth inequality 26-28, 30, 45, 53, 73, 77; in Britain 12, 26, 28; in France 28; in USA 28
India 5, 18, 20, 26, 31, 33, 73
Indonesia 18
industrialisation 6-10, 13, 16, 18, 31, 54, 55, 59, 62, 70
'industrial reserve army' of labour 16
industrial workers 7-9, 16, 31, 32, 35, 56, 72, 76
inequality, gender 7-12; global 26, 31, 32; see income and wealth inequality
inflation 45, 46, 47, 64
innovation 15, 71, 77
interest on capital 4, 5, 24, 27, 28, 35, 45, 47, 48-50, 63, 73
Inter-Governmental Panel on Climate Change, UN 56
International Confederation of Trade Unions 30
International Labour Organisation (ILO) 13, 14, 82, 83, 84, 88, 89
International Monetary Fund (IMF) 49, 50, 53, 83
International Working Men's Association (IWMA, 'First International') 1, 5, 10
investment, capital 1, 2, 5, 14, 16, 24, 27, 37, 39, 42, 45, 47, 48, 52, 57, 59, 63-66, 68, 70, 71, 79
Ireland 12, 17, 30

iron and steel industry 7, 15, 24
Italy 1, 20, 30, 33, 63, 64

J

Jamaica 5
Japan 12, 20, 39, 42, 46, 63, 64, 68
Jones, Peter 43

K

Kalogerakos, Themistoklis 43, 52
Kasmir, Sharryn 73
Kautsky, Karl 1, 19
Kenya 5
Keynes, John Maynard or 'Keynesianism' 33, 34, 45-47; 'military Keynesianism' 46; left-Keynesians 45, 46
Khanin, GI 88
Khrushchev, Nikita 64
Kidron, Michael 46
Kondratiev, Nikolai 15
Korea, North (DPRK) 65
Kosygin, Alexei 63, 65

L

labour, 'simple' 44
labour, certificates or tokens 58, 75; collective or social 18, 19, 25, 34, 35, 60, 61, 72, 81; complex 44; flexibility 10, 17, 19, 50, 53; living 3-6, 13, 14, 37, 38, 40, 52, 55, 59; market 11, 46, 53, 79; necessary 3, 6, 36, 37, 62, 63; past 3, 6, 13; process 6, 13, 14, 29; productive or non-productive 34-36, 43, 85; productivity 6, 16, 38-40, 51, 53, 58-60, 64, 66, 68, 75, 80; surplus (unpaid) 3, 6, 7, 32, 35, 36, 48, 58, 60, 62, 63, 66, 67, 76, 80
Labour Party 29, 42, 47, 50, 80, 85
labour power 2-9, 13, 14, 16, 17, 34, 36-40, 43, 45, 48, 54, 56, 58, 59, 62, 64, 66, 69, 78
Labour Theory of Value 2, 3, 37; see Surplus Value, Marxist Theory of
labour time, value creation by 3-6, 37, 60, 63
landowners 4, 17, 18, 32, 61, 70, 73
Law of Value, Marx's 62, 63, 67, 68
Lehman Brothers 50
leisure time 3, 10, 59
Lenin, Vladimir Ilyich 19, 25, 62, 67, 70, 75
Li, Minqi 42, 79
Lloyd George, David 43,44
London, City of 24, 49-51, 80
London, domestic servants 9; garment workers 8
long waves or cycles, economic 15, 16, 29, 41, 42, 46, 52
luxury commodities 37, 39

M

machinery 2, 4, 6-10, 13, 14, 17, 18, 29, 38, 39, 42, 54, 55, 59, 64, 77
Maito, Esteban 41, 42
managers and management 27, 28, 39, 48, 66, 73, 74, 76-78
Manchester, University of 33
Manchuria 68
Mandel, Ernest 62
Maoism 66, 69
market forces 2, 3, 15, 33, 37, 38, 45, 46-48, 53, 56, 59, 62, 73, 74, 79
Marshall, Alfred 33, 34
Marshall Plan 45

means of consumption or subsistence 3, 31, 37, 38, 45, 54, 58, 59, 62
means of distribution 23, 24, 32, 35, 75, 78
means of exchange 21, 32, 35, 47, 48, 72, 75, 78
means of production 2-6, 14, 16-19, 25, 32, 37-40, 58, 59, 61-63, 66, 67, 69, 74, 75, 78
mechanisation 13, 16, 17, 38-40, 56, 59
merchant's capital or profit 18, 35, 47, 48, 52, 75
mergers and acquisitions 25, 50, 53
metal industries 7, 9, 15, 24
Mexico 18, 73
Middle East 11, 12
migrant workers and migration 12, 17, 31, 53
militarism 17, 25, 32, 46, 47, 67, 78
military expenditure 46, 63, 64, 68
Mill, John Stuart 32
mills, textile 7, 8, 10
modes of production, 1, 32, 54; capitalist 1, 2, 10, 11, 15, 17-19, 25, 34, 36, 40, 43, 54, 55, 60, 61, 67, 73, 79; communist 57-62, 67, 72, 74, 77, 79; feudal 1, 17, 19; slave 1, 19
Mondragon Cooperative Corporation 73, 74
monetarism 29, 33, 41, 46, 47
money 1, 2, 4, 17, 34-36, 45-51, 56, 58, 59, 69
money-capital 36, 47, 48, 49, 59
money markets 49, 59
money supply 46, 47
monopolies, capitalist 19, 20, 23-25, 53, 57, 67, 74
monopolisation 19, 20, 23, 24, 32, 57
Morrisson, Christian 26, 83, 84

N
National Coal Board 78
National Debt 17, 18, 45, 52
nationalisation, capitalist 45, 50, 51, 61, 67; socialist 45, 50, 61, 67, 70, 71, 75, 76
National Union of Mineworkers 78
Nazism 66, 67, 68
nature, forces of 19, 54, 60, 61
neo-liberalism 31, 33, 41, 47, 49, 52, 53
Netherlands (Holland) 12, 17, 30, 42
New Deal, the 45
New Economic Policy 62, 70
New Labour 47, 50
New Lanark 58
new technology 39, 47, 80
New York Daily Tribune 2
Nigeria 5
night work 8, 10, 13
Northern Rock 50
Norway 44
nutrition 9, 30, 31, 60

O
October Socialist Revolution 5, 62, 75, 78
Office for National Statistics 12, 27, 41
oligarchy, financial 19, 24
Opium Wars 17
Organisation for Economic Co-operation and Development 39
over-accumulation of capital 14-15, 40, 45, 49, 51, 52, 53
over-production of commodities 2, 14-15, 40, 45, 49, 51, 52, 59
Owen, Robert or 'Owenism' 11, 58, 61, 72, 73, 75

P

Pakistan 5
Panama and Paradise Papers 28
paper-making industry 8
Paris Agreement on Climate Change 57
part-time workers 12, 30, 53
pauperisation or immiseration 25, 26, 29, 31
peasantry 17, 19, 31, 55, 69, 75
pensions 13, 27, 28, 50, 53, 78
'Permanent Arms Economy', theory of 46
physiocrats 32
piece-work 3, 66
planning, socialist or communist 18, 30, 58, 59, 63, 64, 65, 67, 69, 70-72, 74, 75, 79-81; see Five Year
    Plans
Poland 1, 12, 30, 63, 65, 75, 76
political economy, bourgeois or capitalist 46; classical 1, 3, 32, 33; Marxist 13, 15, 33, 34, 37, 38, 66, 67,
    78, 85; neo-classical 33; neo-liberal 33, 34, 46, 47, 53; see Keynes
Portugal 5, 18, 20, 30
poverty 9, 12, 30-32, 45, 65, 71
Preobrazhensky, Yevgeni 62
price formation, capitalist 3, 4, 6, 14, 36-39, 44, 48, 51, 56, 60; socialist 62, 63, 64, 65, 66, 68
price of production 37, 38, 44
privatisation 33, 46, 47, 50, 59, 65, 77
Privy Council 7
productivity, capitalist 6, 16, 38-40, 51, 52, 53; socialist or communist 58-60, 64, 66, 68, 75, 80
profit, capitalist 2, 4, 5, 14, 18, 24, 29, 35-37, 40, 46, 48, 49, 52, 53, 54, 58, 59, 60, 63, 69, 73;
    commercial 35, 36, 47, 48; mass of 16, 24, 36, 39, 47, 53; maximisation of (surplus value) 5, 6, 8, 14,
    40, 66, 68, 78; merchant's 18, 47, 52; rate of 19, 38-44, 46, 47, 51-53;
Proudhon, Pierre-Joseph 75
Public and Commercial Services (PCS) union 28
public expenditure 6, 45, 46, 50, 51, 57
public or social ownership 23, 30, 46, 59, 61-63, 65, 67, 69-74, 76, 77, 79, 80
public sector or workers in 12, 34, 36, 70, 71, 75, 76
public services 6, 12, 34, 36, 45
purchasing power, workers' 5-6, 14, 40, 45, 52
'putting-out' system 9

R

railways 1, 5, 15, 18, 24, 48, 59
recession, capitalist 2, 14-16, 26, 33, 37, 40, 45-47, 51-53, 73
recovery, capitalist 2, 14, 42, 43, 52
'Reform and Opening Up' 70
relations of production 1, 32, 33, 60, 72, 78
rent 4, 5, 27, 28, 35, 43, 52, 61
'reserve army', industrial 16, 17
retail sector 12, 20, 23, 24, 35, 48, 63, 73, 75
revolution, socialist 1, 5, 62, 70, 72, 75, 77, 78, 79
Ricardo, David 2, 3, 32, 34
Roberts, Michael 4, 40-43
Robinson, Joan 34, 46
robotics 39
Roosevelt, Franklin D 45
Rumania 68
rural economy 9, 17, 18, 31, 56, 70, 71, 75, 76, 77
Russia or Soviet Union 5, 12, 15, 30, 33, 49, 54, 62-70, 75, 77, 79, 87-89

S

sanitation 60
science and scientists 36, 54, 57, 81
Second (Socialist) International 5
Second World War 16, 17, 28, 29, 41, 65, 66, 68, 75, 77
securities, financial 48, 50, 51
self-employment 6, 27, 76
semi-colonialism 19, 25
services sector 2, 12, 23, 24, 29, 30, 34-36, 48, 58, 64, 76, 77
sexual harassment 12
skilled workers 6, 7, 9, 11, 13, 36, 44, 75
slavery 7, 10, 25, 26, 32, 39; mode of production 1, 9, 19; slave trade 18, 18, 31
Slovakia 12, 30
Slovenia 12
slowdown, capitalist 14, 15, 47, 68; see recession
Smith, Adam 2, 3, 32, 34, 46, 67
social and welfare policy 6, 12, 13, 18, 41, 42, 45, 47, 53, 66
'social capital' 53
social democracy 12, 30, 47
social *or* collective labour 18, 19, 25, 34, 35, 60, 61, 72
socialism 62, 67, 81; and China 18, 30, 70-72, 81; and Cuba 65, 77, 78, 81; and Eastern Europe 30, 33,
    49, 63-65, 66, 75-77, 78, 79; and Soviet Union 30, 33, 62, 66-69, 75, 78; and Vietnam 65, 78
Socialist International 5
socialist ownership 62, 71, 72, 74, 80; see nationalisation
social or welfare benefits 6, 13, 29, 30, 41, 42, 50
'social wage' 6, 13, 41, 42, 53, 66
South Africa 79
Soviet Union or Russia 5, 12, 15, 30, 33, 49, 54, 62-70, 75, 77, 79, 87-89
Spain 12, 17, 18, 21, 30, 73
speculation, financial 1, 2, 14, 15, 48-51, 59
Stalin, Josef 62, 63, 67, 70, 88
'Stalinism' 66-68
state capitalism 66, 67, 69, 70
state-monopoly capitalism 25, 29, 56, 67, 80
state power, capitalist 17, 20, 47, 49, 74, 79; socialist 62, 66, 67, 75, 76, 79, 81
stocks and shares 1, 2, 24, 28, 48, 52, 70, 71
strikes 5, 17, 74
subsistence or consumption, means of 37, 38, 45, 54, 58, 59
Sukachev, Vladimir 54
super-exploitation of labour 13, 19, 53
super-profits 19
superstructure, society's 32
supervisory work 39, 73
supply and demand 3, 33, 63, 79
surplus value 1-6, 13, 14, 16, 29, 34-40, 42-45, 48, 49, 52, 60, 62, 63, 66, 68, 69, 73, 77, 78, 85; Marxist
    theory of 1, 2, 42, 43, 44, 49; maximisation of 5, 6, 8, 14, 40, 66, 68, 78
sustainable development 61, 71, 77, 80, 81
Sweden 12, 42, 46
Switzerland 20, 28, 44

T

taxation 6, 17, 18, 27, 28, 43-45, 46, 47, 53, 63, 77; avoidance or evasion 28, 45, 77, 84
teachers 34, 45
technical work 29
technological advance 14-16, 24, 36, 39, 47, 54, 55, 57, 62, 64, 68-70, 76, 79, 80, 81
telecommunications 23, 72
Temporal Single-System Interpretation 44, 52

temporary work 17, 30, 73
Tendency of the Rate of Profit to Fall (TRPF) 38-40, 42-44, 47, 51, 52, 53
textile workers 7-10, 16
'Thatcherism' 47
Third World or developing countries 18, 31, 42, 47, 51, 65, 68; debt 31
Tomlinson, Dan 24
tools 16, 17, 19, 38, 42, 54, 55
Tory government 47
Trades Union Congress 11, 14
trade unions 5, 7, 11-14, 28-30, 34, 41, 42, 43, 46, 47, 53, 66, 74, 78, 80; density 12, 30, 74; women and 11-13, 30
trafficking of children 7; women 12
training 13, 36, 45, 53
transnational corporations (TNCs) 13, 20-23, 71
transport 23, 24, 35, 47, 57, 66, 70-72
'Troika', the 50
Trotsky, Leon 66
Turkey 33

U

Ukraine 30, 68
under-consumptionism, theories of 45, 46
unemployment or the unemployed 11, 13, 16, 17, 31, 40, 65
United Nations 56, 81; Inter-Governmental Panel on Climate Change 56
United States of America 1, 2, 4, 12, 13, 15, 16, 18-20, 24, 28, 29, 33, 39, 42, 43, 45-47, 49-52, 57, 63, 64, 65, 71, 72, 73, 74
United Steelworkers of the USA 74
universities 33, 34
unskilled workers 7, 11, 29, 35, 36, 39
urban workers 17, 18, 64, 72, 76
Uruguay 30
use-value 3, 4, 35, 36, 56, 69
usury 47
'Utopian Socialism' 58, 72, 75

V

value: exchange-value 2-4, 6, 34, 35, 37, 38, 48, 56, 60, 62, 63, 68, 69; surplus value 1-6, 13, 14, 16, 29, 34-40, 42-45, 48, 49, 52, 60, 62, 63, 66, 68, 69, 73, 77, 78, 85; use-value 3, 4, 35, 36, 56, 69
Venezuela 79
Vernadsky, Vladimir 54
Vietnam 65, 78

W

wage, equivalent value of 3, 35, 36
wage-capital 14, 38, 43
Wages, Price and Profit 29
'wages for housework' 13
Walkley. Mary Anne 8
wealth, distribution of 27, 28, 32, 43-45, 77, 85; taxation of 28, 43-45, 85
well-being, human 26, 31, 60, 81
Western Europe 1, 11, 15, 18, 42, 44, 45, 63, 64
West Indies 18, 63, 64
women workers 6-13, 30, 32, 59; and equal pay 11-13; super-exploitation of 13; trade unionism among 11-13, 30
work process 6, 13, 14, 29
Working Time Directive 5

World Bank 30, 31, 49, 53
World Development Report (2019) 53
World Federation of Trade Unions 30
World Trade Organisation 49, 71
World War One 25, 26, 27, 28, 41, 67
World War Two 16, 17, 28, 29, 41, 65, 66, 68, 75, 77

Y

young workers 7-10, 12, 39
Yugoslavia 77

Z

Zedong, Mao 66
zero-hour contracts 17, 53

www.ingramcontent.com/pod-product-compliance
Lightning Source LLC
Chambersburg PA
CBHW052139270326
41930CB00012B/2950

* 9 7 8 1 9 0 7 4 6 4 3 6 2 *